GUIDE TO
MICROWAVE
COOKING

Ideals Publishing Corp.
Milwaukee, Wisconsin

Contents

All recipes are prepared on full cycle, or "high," unless otherwise specified. For convenience, recipes are cycle coded as follows:

Cover recipes:
Beef Roll-Ups, page 32
Spanish Rice, page 25
Corn Relish, page 25
Candied Carrots, page 25
Cinnamon Puffs, page 41
Fruit Frost, page 8
Lime Soufflé, page 49

Pictured above are the dishes and utensils safe to use in a microwave. The picture at the bottom right is the Amana Radarange Model RR-10 used to test these recipes.

Introduction

The age of the microwave is here. What was once a second cousin to the conventional oven has come into its own. There was a time when microwave ovens were thought useful only for reheating leftovers; but as the homemaker's busy schedule became more crowded, the microwave became a respectable and, to many, an indispensible appliance. Here are a few of the reasons why so many modern families cook the microwave way:

Speed: Food cooks on an average of four times faster than in conventional ovens.

Cleanliness: Since the oven walls stay cool, cleanups are simply a matter of wiping spills with a damp cloth.

Energy-saving: Compared to conventional ovens, microwave ovens use less power for a shorter period of time.

Money-saving: On the average, a microwave oven uses about 14 percent of the electricity of a conventional oven.

Health: The shorter cooking time for most foods results in a retention of vitamins and minerals lost through conventional cooking methods. Food is tastier, too.

The advantages of a microwave oven are easily seen; however, as in any new skill, learning to cook the microwave way takes practice and perhaps a little patience. We suggest you first read your owner's manual thoroughly before beginning. Then, use your oven, not just for reheating food, but for preparing entire meals. You'll find mealtimes are happier, healthier and much less hectic.

Microwave ovens are available in a variety of models made by several manufacturers. All perform well and are manufactured in accordance with strict safety standards. These recipes were tested using the Amana Radarange Model RR-10. Unless otherwise indicated, all recipes are cooked on the "High" or "Full" power setting.

How Does It Work?

Microwaves are electromagnetic waves, similar to radio and television waves, only much shorter — about the length of a ballpoint pen. Since they are non-ionizing rays, which means they do not

3

produce any chemical changes, they are safe. Produced by a magnetron tube, microwaves are emitted into the oven where they are set in motion by a stirrer fan. There will be some spots in the oven that get more microwaves than other spots; and, for this reason, food must be turned periodically for even cooking. (Instead of a fan, some ovens have a turntable on the bottom which continually turns the food while cooking.)

In microwave ovens, the microwaves hit water molecules, basic ingredients in all foods, which start vibrating. (Fat molecules are also sensitive to microwaves.) These molecules vibrate against each other, thus cooking the food. In contrast, a conventional oven must heat the air which in turn gradually penetrates the food.

The microwaves enter from the outside of the food, travel through the food, losing half their power every ¾ inch. Continued cooking to the center occurs mainly by conduction. That is, vibrating molecules bounce against their neighbors and cause them to vibrate. This is why food cooks from the outside toward the center.

What Dishes to Use

Microwaves easily penetrate food, but they cannot penetrate metal. That is why it is important to use the proper utensils in your oven — those which allow microwaves to pass through the food — and why shielding food, such as turkey wings and cakes, will prevent portions of it from cooking. Glassware is perfect to use, as are china and ceramic plates and casseroles — if they contain no metal. Although paper and plastic containers are good for quick reheating, for prolonged cooking the containers must be able to withstand high temperatures produced by the food. Plastic cooking pouches are excellent for use in the microwave, but a slit must be made in the top for steam to escape.

Test Your Utensils First

Dishes can be tested for their suitability in a microwave oven. Fill a one-cup glass measure and set it into the dish in question. Place the dish in the oven and turn the setting to full power for one-and-a-half to two minutes. If the water gets hot but the dish stays cool, it can be safely used in the microwave oven.

If the dish "sparks," don't be alarmed. Turn off the oven immediately and transfer the food to another dish. The sparks indicate there is metal in the dish being tested and it is not safe for the oven.

Covering and Shielding

Food is often covered before cooking in the microwave oven. This helps retain moisture and prevent splattering. Plastic wrap and waxed paper make excellent coverings, or a casserole cover or dinner plate may be used. Some manufacturers allow the use of small pieces of aluminum foil to shield portions of food which otherwise overcook. Check the introductions to the meat and cake sections for directions on shielding and check your instruction manual for the proper use of foil in your particular oven.

Season Food after Cooking

Do not season food before it is cooked in a microwave oven. Food is naturally tasty; but in conventional ovens, much of that natural flavor is lost due to prolonged cooking. The speed with which the microwave cooks preserves this natural flavor. Salt, however, distorts the cooking pattern of the microwaves and will result in a drier and tougher finished product. If you must have salt in your food, use it after cooking.

Browning in a Microwave

Since microwave ovens do not use heat, food does not brown as in an ordinary oven. There is one very specialized dish called a browning skillet or dish which is handy to have for cooking fast-frying items, such as fried eggs and grilled sandwiches. Because of a special metal oxide encased in the bottom of this skillet, it gets very hot when heated empty in the oven. The time needed for preheating is determined by the density of the item and experience is really the best teacher. By using this skillet, foods such as steaks, chops and even bread can be browned (see page 40).

Be a Clockwatcher

Since foods do cook quickly, timing is critical with a microwave oven. A mere few seconds may make the difference between beautiful, light-as-air cupcakes and stone-hard objects suitable for hockey pucks. The starting temperature of the food itself also affects its cooking time. Food right from the refrigerator requires an additional minute or minute and a half cooking time than if the food is at room temperature when microwaved. Until you are thoroughly familar with your oven, use the minimum amount of time given in the recipe. You can always add more cooking time later.

Food also continues to cook after it is removed from the oven. That is the reason recipes often direct you to "let stand" several minutes after the cooking time is up. This "standing time" or "carryover cooking" then finishes cooking food to the right degree.

Food cooks about four times faster in a microwave oven than in a conventional oven. This, however, is not a hard and fast rule as the nature and density of the food affects its cooking time. The best way to accurately judge the amount of time needed for a recipe is to find a similar recipe in a microwave cookbook, such as this one. When doubling recipes, however, use one and one-half times the cooking time recommended.

Another factor which affects cooking time is the power of your oven. The recipes in this book were tested using a 650 to 675-watt oven. Ovens with less power need additional time in the following amounts:

600-700 Watts	500-600 Watts	400-500 Watts
15 sec.	17 sec.	20 sec.
30 sec.	35 sec.	41 sec.
1 min.	1 min. 9 sec.	1 min. 21 sec.
2 min.	2 min. 22 sec.	2 min. 42 sec.
3 min.	3 min. 27 sec.	4 min. 3 sec.
4 min.	4 min. 36 sec.	5 min. 24 sec.
5 min.	5 min. 45 sec.	6 min. 45 sec.
10 min.	11 min. 30 sec.	13 min. 30 sec.
15 min.	17 min. 15 sec.	20 min. 15 sec.
20 min.	23 min.	27 min.
25 min.	25 min. 45 sec.	33 min. 45 sec.
30 min.	34 min. 30 sec.	40 min. 30 sec.

Reheating Food

Microwave ovens can definitely be used to reheat yesterday's dinner or even breakfast. As in a conventional oven, cover most items except those which should be crispy. Pancakes from the early riser are still delicious for the sleepy heads if you first spread on butter and syrup before placing in the oven. Cover with plastic wrap, microwave on high for 45 seconds to 1 minute (if refrigerator cold, for 1 to 1½ minutes) and serve hot pancakes topped with melted butter and steaming syrup.

The defrost cycle is perfect for reheating delicate egg and cheese dishes. This cycle automatically shuts off at 30-second intervals, thus ensuring a gentle heating process. Reheat food 2 minutes on defrost rather than 1 minute on high. Because of the automatic shutoff, the total microwave time is the same.

Shapes and places

How food is placed in the microwave oven is very important. Because food cooks first around the outside edges, position the heavier portions around the outside of the dish. For instance, chicken drumsticks should be placed with the thick end toward the edge and the thinner part toward the center. Arrange broccoli with the stalk out and the flower inside.

The center of the dish should be left empty, except when cooking one item. This is especially true in baking. For instance, bake twelve cookies at a time, placing them around the outer edges of a round cookie sheet; bake cakes in a tube pan or in a bundt pan. Regular glass or plastic cake pans can be used or even mixing bowls by inverting a jelly glass or tumbler in the center. When cooking only one item, place it in the center of the oven.

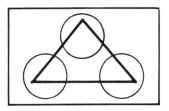

If cooking two or more items, set at least one inch apart.

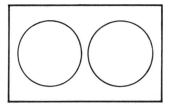

Three items, set in the angles of an imaginary triangle.

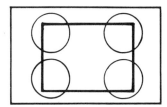

With four items, set them at the corners of a square.

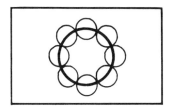

Place five or more items in a circle, leaving the center free.

It's the Modern Way

Now that you have the basics, go ahead—plan tonight's dinner and cook it in your microwave oven. Use the recipes you find in this book—they are all clear and easy-to-follow. Enjoy the pleasure of fast and efficient meal preparation—the microwave way.

Appetizers

Parties are a snap when you have a microwave oven. Prepare your dips and fillings early in the day; then, at party time, simply pop them in the oven for last-minute reheating. Most foods will heat in just 30 to 60 seconds. When reheating delicate items, such as cheese and mushrooms, use the medium cycle and cover food with plastic wrap. Appetizers made on crackers or toast should be spread at the last minute to avoid a soggy base. To cook canapés, arrange in a curve and turn dish after half the cooking time is up.

PECAN SPREAD

1 8-oz. pkg. cream cheese
2 T. milk
¼ c. chopped green pepper
½ t. garlic salt
¼ t. pepper
2 T. dry onion flakes
½ c. sour cream
1 T. melted butter
½ c. chopped pecans
½ t. salt

Place cream cheese in a bowl and microwave 30 to 45 seconds. Add milk, green pepper, garlic salt, pepper, onion flakes and sour cream; mix well. Microwave butter 15 seconds to melt; stir in pecans and salt. Sprinkle buttered pecans over cheese mixture. Serve with crackers. Serves 12.

SMOKY CHEESE BALL /HIGH

1 8-oz. pkg. cream cheese
1 roll smoke-flavored cheese spread
1 t. Worcestershire sauce
1 c. chopped pecans
½ c. chopped parsley

Place cheeses in a 1½-quart casserole. Microwave 1 minute. Add Worcestershire sauce and mix. Chill 30 minutes in freezer. Form into a ball. Roll in pecans, then in chopped parsley. Chill. Serve with crackers.

NOTE: Any flavor of cheese can be substituted for variety. Serves 12.

SNACK NIBBLES

½ c. butter
1 T. Nature's Seasonings spice
3 T. Worcestershire sauce
1 6-oz. pkg. pretzel sticks
1 8-oz. can peanuts
2 c. Wheat Chex
2 c. Rice Chex
2 c. Cheerios

Microwave butter 45 seconds to melt; stir in Nature's Seasonings spice and Worcestershire sauce. Mix well. Pour over remaining ingredients in a 3-quart dish. Microwave 6 minutes, stirring every 2 minutes. Serves 8.

APPETIZER MEATBALLS

1 lb. ground chuck
1 onion, finely chopped
¾ t. salt
1 10½-oz. can tomato soup
3 T. lemon juice
¼ c. brown sugar
1 1-lb. can pineapple chunks, drained

Form 1-inch balls from ground chuck. In a 9-inch square dish, combine onion, salt, soup, lemon juice and brown sugar. Cover and microwave 7 minutes, stirring twice. Add meatballs to sauce. Microwave 5 to 6 minutes, covered, stirring twice. Add chunks; heat 1 minute. Serves 6.

Pictured opposite, clockwise from left
Pecan spread
Mixture for Bacon-Cheese Puffs (page 9)
Smoky Cheese Ball

MINI PIZZAS HIGH

1 6-oz. can tomato paste
  Snack crackers
  Oregano
1 4-oz. pkg. pepperoni slices
1 6-oz. pkg. mozzarella slices

Spread tomato paste on crackers; sprinkle with oregano. Top with pepperoni and cheese. Place 12 crackers at a time in a circle on a paper plate. Microwave 45 seconds. Turn dish one-half turn after 20 seconds. Serve hot. Serves 16.

WARM BLOODY MARY MED

4 c. tomato juice
1 t. Worcestershire sauce
¼ t. salt
¼ t. oregano
¼ t. marjoram
3 whole cloves
¼ c. butter
½ c. vodka

Combine all ingredients in 1½-quart bowl. Microwave 3½ minutes on medium. Stir twice; don't boil. Remove cloves and serve. Makes 1 quart.

CHEESE PRETZELS HIGH

1 8-oz. pkg. processed American cheese
¼ c. light cream
½ t. Tabasco sauce
1 pkg. pretzels
1 T. poppy seed

Cut cheese into pieces. Place cheese, cream and Tabasco into a casserole. Microwave 2 to 3 minutes. Stir smooth each minute. Dip half of pretzel into cheese. Sprinkle with poppy seed. Place on waxed paper until firm. Serves 8.

FRUIT FROST HIGH

1½ c. lemon juice
1½ c. sugar
1 qt. orange juice
1 qt. ginger ale
  Mint sprigs for garnish

Combine lemon juice and sugar in a 1-quart casserole. Microwave 4 minutes. Stir lemon juice into orange juice. Pour into ice-cube trays and freeze. To serve, place 4 cubes in each glass. Crush slightly with a fork. Fill with cold ginger ale. Garnish with mint. Serves 6.

HOT MINTY CHOCOLATE HIGH

5 T. cocoa
5 T. sugar
⅛ t. salt
½ c. water
3 c. milk
½ t. vanilla
  Peppermint schnapps to taste

Mix cocoa, sugar and salt in a 2-quart bowl. Blend in water. Microwave 2 minutes to boiling. Stir well. Add milk, vanilla and peppermint schnapps. Microwave 5 to 6 minutes on medium cycle. Do not boil. Makes 8 servings.

RASPBERRY COOLER HIGH

2 12-oz. pkgs. frozen raspberries
½ c. sugar
1½ c. lemonade
2 c. orange juice
2 c. ice water
1 qt. ginger ale, chilled

Combine 1 package raspberries with sugar in a 2-cup measure. Microwave on medium 4 minutes. Crush berries. Combine remaining ingredients in a large bowl. Add crushed raspberries. Just before serving, add ginger ale and 1 package uncrushed thawed raspberries. Serves 6.

DELIGHTFUL CRAB DIP

1 8-oz. pkg. softened cream cheese
⅓ c. mayonnaise
1 t. creamy horseradish
1½ T. minced onion
½ t. seasoned salt
1 T. chopped parsley
Dash garlic powder
1 6-oz. pkg. chopped crab meat

Blend cream cheese, mayonnaise, horseradish, onion and seasoned salt. Fold in parsley, garlic powder and crab meat. Serve well chilled with fresh vegetables and crackers or serve hot. To heat, place in microwave oven for 1½ minutes. Stir and heat another 1 to 1½ minutes. Serves 12.

NOTE: If the cream cheese is refrigerator cold, unwrap it from foil, place on a plate and microwave for 30 to 45 seconds. This will bring the cheese to room temperature.

To get more juice from citrus fruits, microwave them, one at a time, 30 seconds before squeezing.

SNACK TIME KABOBS

1 15-oz. can Spam
1 1-lb. can pinneapple chunks
1 T. brown sugar
2 T. soy sauce
1 T. vinegar
Toothpicks

Cut meat into 60 cubes. Drain pineapple chunks and cut in half. Place one of each on a toothpick. Arrange in a single layer in dish. Combine sauce ingredients and spoon over kabobs. Marinate 1 hour. Transfer to platter. Cook 30 at a time for 2 minutes. Turn dish one-half turn; spoon sauce over kabobs; and cook 1¾ minutes. Makes 60 kabobs.

SPICED CIDER

2 qts. apple juice
4 whole cinnamon sticks
16 whole allspice
16 whole cloves
2 T. brown sugar
2 lemons, sliced
2 oranges, sliced

In a 3-quart bowl, combine all ingredients. Microwave 15 minutes, uncovered. Stir; let stand 15 to 60 minutes. Remove spices. Serve warm. Makes 2 quarts.

BACON-CHEESE PUFFS

2 8-oz. pkgs. softened cream cheese
1 egg yolk
1 t. instant minced onion
1 t. baking powder
2½ T. imitation bacon pieces
60 round snack crackers

Combine cream cheese, egg yolk, and onion in a large bowl; beat well. Add baking powder and bacon pieces. Mix well. Place 6 crackers at a time in a circle on a paper plate. Top each cracker with 1 teaspoon cheese mixture. Heat on medium 1 to 1½ minutes. Serve hot. Makes about 60 puffs.

BEEF AND CHEESE APPETIZERS

1 4-oz. pkg. sliced smoked beef
1 c. shredded Cheddar cheese
1 can pitted ripe olives, drained and sliced
1 c. mayonnaise
1 8-oz. pkg. rye crackers

Combine smoked beef, cheese, olives and mayonnaise, blending well. Spread 1 tablespoon on each cracker. Microwave, 6 crackers at a time, 45 seconds, turning dish one-half turn after 22 seconds. Makes 12 servings.

NOTE: Appetizers may be frozen. Heat frozen appetizers 1½ minutes.

Fruit and Salad

Fruits maintain their color and shape when cooked in a microwave. Dried fruits may be rehydrated quickly in the microwave. Raisins can be plumped or apples turned into sauce in a jiffy. Test fruits after half the allotted cooking time since ripeness of the fruit affects cooking time.

To facilitate the preparation of salad dressings, and all sauces and gravies, mix them in a four-cup glass measure with a pouring lip. If the dressing contains mayonnaise, microwave on medium cycle to avoid separation. The standing time in sauce recipes allows the sauce to heat through to the center.

HOT SPINACH SALAD

4 slices bacon
1 clove garlic, minced
¼ c. red wine vinegar
2 T. soy sauce
   Dash pepper
1 can water chestnuts, drained and sliced
3 green onions, sliced
¾ lb. fresh spinach

Place bacon on bacon grid; cover with paper toweling. Microwave approximately 2½ minutes; set bacon aside. Combine drippings and remaining ingredients except spinach. Tear spinach into bite-size pieces. Microwave dressing 1 to 1½ minutes to boiling. Stir after 45 seconds. Pour dressing over spinach; toss to coat all spinach pieces. Crumble bacon over top. Serve immediately. Serves 6.

CHICKEN PEACH SALAD

1 10-oz. pkg. frozen rice pilaf
¼ c. mayonnaise
1 T. chopped onion
½ c. chopped celery
½ t. curry
1½ c. canned peaches, drained and chopped
2 c. cubed, cooked chicken
¼ c. chopped green pepper
   Sliced almonds for garnish

Puncture frozen rice pouch and place in the oven. Microwave 3½ minutes or until thawed; let stand 2 minutes. Place rice into a serving bowl and cool. Add mayonnaise, onion, celery, curry, peaches and chicken. Chill. Stir in green pepper just before serving. Garnish with sliced almonds. Serves 4 to 6.

Pictured opposite
Cole Slaw Soufflé
(page 12)

COTTAGE LIME SALAD HIGH

2 3-oz. pkgs. lemon gelatin
2 3-oz. pkgs. lime gelatin
4 c. water
1 c. mayonnaise
3 c. creamed small-curd cottage cheese
1 c. crushed pineapple
⅔ c. evaporated milk
1 c. chopped pecans

Place water and gelatin in a large bowl; stir. Microwave 4 to 6 minutes, or until mixture boils. Chill until thickened. Add mayonnaise and blend. Stir in remaining ingredients. Spoon into a 12-cup mold. Chill. Unmold and garnish with thin slices of twisted lime. Serves 8.

CLASSIC DRESSING HIGH MED

1 c. milk	¼ t. paprika
1 T. cornstarch	¼ t. pepper
2 t. sugar	1 egg yolk, beaten
1 t. dry mustard	2 T. vinegar
1 t. salt	¼ c. vegetable oil

Pour milk into a 4-cup glass measure. Blend in cornstarch, sugar, mustard, salt, paprika and pepper, mixing well. Microwave 3 minutes; beat smooth. Microwave 1 to 1½ minutes until thick, stirring after 30 seconds; beat smooth. Stir a little of the warm mixture into egg yolk. Then pour egg yolk into hot mixture. Microwave on medium 1 to 2 minutes until thick. Stir in vinegar and oil; beat smooth. Cool. Makes 1½ cups.

CREAMY DRESSING MED

2 eggs, well beaten
¼ c. sugar
¼ c. orange juice
¼ c. lemon juice
¼ t. salt
½ c. heavy cream, whipped

Beat eggs in a 4-cup glass measure. Stir in sugar, orange juice, lemon juice and salt. Mix well. Microwave on medium 3 minutes, stirring after 1½ minutes. Beat until smooth. Microwave on medium 2 to 3 minutes until thick. Beat until smooth. Chill. Fold into whipped cream. Serve over fruit. Makes 1½ cups.

COLE SLAW SOUFFLÉ HIGH

1 8-oz. can crushed pineapple
1 3-oz. pkg. orange gelatin
¾ c. water
¾ c. mayonnaise
1 c. finely shredded cabbage
1 c. shredded carrot
½ c. raisins
½ c. chopped walnuts
3 egg whites, beaten stiff

Fold a 22-inch piece of aluminum foil in half lengthwise. Tape around a 1-quart soufflé dish. Drain pineapple, reserving juice. Combine water, reserved juice and gelatin in a mixing bowl. Microwave 2½ to 3 minutes, until boiling. Beat in mayonnaise. Place in a cold loaf pan; freeze about 20 minutes until firm at the edge but still soft in the center. Pour in a large bowl and beat until fluffy. Fold in pineapple. Add remaining ingredients and pour into the prepared soufflé dish. Chill. Remove foil and serve. Serves 8.

APPLESAUCE HIGH

4 c. peeled apple slices
½ c. water
½ c. sugar
¼ t. cinnamon

Place apples, water and sugar in a deep 1½-quart bowl. Cover and microwave 8 to 9 minutes. Add cinnamon while hot. Puree in blender if a smooth sauce is desired. Serves 4 to 6.

CARAMEL APPLES HIGH

5 to 6 medium apples
5 to 6 wooden skewers
1 lb. caramels
1 T. water
Chopped nuts

Wash and dry apples. Insert skewers. Place caramels and water in a deep narrow glass bowl. Microwave 2 minutes. Stir until smooth. Dip apples into caramel mixture. Twirl to coat and dip into chopped nuts. Place on buttered waxed paper. If caramel mixture becomes too stiff, microwave another 20 seconds. Enough for 5 or 6 apples.

CRANBERRY-PINEAPPLE MOLD

1½ c. water
1 6-oz. pkg. cherry gelatin
1 11-oz. can mandarin oranges
1 8-oz. can crushed pineapple
1 can whole cranberry sauce
¼ c. mayonnaise
¼ c. sour cream

Combine water and gelatin in a 4-cup measure. Microwave to boiling, 2½ to 4½ minutes. Drain oranges and pineapple, reserving juice. Add enough water to make 1 cup. Add to gelatin; stir in cranberry sauce. Chill until thickened. Combine mayonnaise and sour cream; stir in 1 cup of the gelatin mixture. Pour sour cream mixture into an 8-cup ring mold; refrigerate to set. Add oranges and pineapple to remaining gelatin. Pour over fruit. Refrigerate 4 hours. Unmold and serve. Serves 8.

HOT AMBROSIA COMPOTE

½ c. flaked coconut
¼ c. graham cracker crumbs
1 1-lb. can pineapple chunks, drained
1 1-lb. can sliced peaches, drained
1 can mandarin oranges, drained
½ c. green grapes
8 maraschino cherries, halved
1 1-lb. can apricots, drained

Combine all ingredients in a 2-quart casserole. Microwave 5 minutes, turning dish one-half turn after 2½ minutes. Cool. Garnish with whipped cream, if desired. Serves 6 to 8.

STRAWBERRY MALLOW

1 3-oz. pkg. strawberry gelatin
2 c. water
2 c. frozen whipped topping, thawed
1 c. miniature marshmallows
1 8-oz. can crushed pineapple, drained

In a 4-cup measure, place gelatin and 1 cup of the water. Microwave 3 to 4 minutes until boiling. Add remaining cup cold water; chill until thickened slightly. Whip with mixer until light and fluffy. Fold in whipped topping, blending well. Fold in marshmallows and pineapple. Pour into serving bowl and chill. Garnish with fresh strawberries. Serves 6 to 8.

DAIQUIRI MOLD

3 3-oz. pkgs. lime gelatin
2¾ c. pineapple syrup plus water
1 12-oz. can frozen limeade concentrate
¼ c. light rum
1 c. mayonnaise
2 20-oz. cans crushed pineapple, drained
2 c. frozen whipped topping, thawed
4 bananas, sliced

Place gelatin and liquid in a large bowl; stir to dissolve. Microwave about 3 to 5 minutes to boiling. Add limeade concentrate and rum. Using mixer, blend in mayonnaise; chill until thickened. Fold in pineapple, whipped topping and bananas. Spoon into a 12-cup mold. Chill until firm. Serves 6 to 8.

For easy peeling, microwave peaches and tomatoes 15 to 20 seconds each, depending on size. Let stand 10 minutes and peel.

CRANBERRY CHEESE MOLD

1 envelope unflavored gelatin
1 c. cold water
1 3-oz. pkg. strawberry gelatin
¾ c. boiling water
1 14-oz. jar cranberry-orange relish
4 T. lemon juice
1 T. grated orange rind
1 8-oz. pkg. cream cheese
1 4½-oz. container whipped topping

Place cold water in a 4-cup measure. Sprinkle unflavored gelatin over water; stir. Microwave 15 to 30 seconds; stir and microwave an additional 15 to 30 seconds. Set aside. Place ¾ cup water and strawberry gelatin in a bowl; stir. Microwave about 2 minutes until it boils; stir. Add cranberry relish, 2 tablespoons lemon juice and orange rind. Pour into a 1½-quart mold; chill. In a bowl, microwave cream cheese 30 to 45 seconds to soften. Beat until fluffy. Beat in remaining 2 tablespoons lemon juice. Blend in topping. Add unflavored gelatin mixture, mixing well. Spoon evenly over cranberry mixture. Chill. Unmold and serve. Makes 8 servings.

CRANBERRIES  High

1½ c. cranberries
½ c. sugar
¼ c. orange juice
1 T. grated orange peel

In a 1-quart casserole, combine all ingredients, stirring to mix. Cover and microwave 3 to 5 minutes until berries pop. Stir after 2 minutes. Let stand, covered, 5 additional minutes. Serves 3 to 4.

BAKED PEARS  High

½ c. cinnamon candies
1 c. apple cider
2 pears
Whipped cream cheese

In an 8-inch glass pie plate, combine candies and cider. Microwave 5 minutes to melt candies. Peel, core and halve pears. Place, cut side down, in cider syrup. Cover and microwave 6 minutes. Turn dish one-quarter turn every 2 minutes. Chill. Garnish with whipped cream cheese. Makes 2 servings.

STRAWBERRY PRESERVES High

1 16-oz. pkg. frozen strawberries
3 T. liquid pectin
2 c. sugar
1 T. lemon juice

Place strawberries in a 2-quart casserole. Microwave 2 minutes. Add pectin and microwave 2 minutes. Add sugar and lemon juice. Microwave 6 minutes, turning dish and stirring every 2 minutes. Pour into glass jars. Cover and refrigerate. Can store in freezer covered with paraffin. Fills 4 to 6 small jars.

BAKED APPLE High

1 apple   ¼ t. cinnamon
1 t. butter   1 t. sugar

Core apple and place in a custard cup. Place butter, cinnamon and sugar in center. Cover with waxed paper and microwave 2 minutes. Let stand, covered, 1 minute. Enough for 1 apple.

STEWED PRUNES High

1½ c. prunes   1 stick cinnamon
2 c. hot water   10 whole allspice
¼ c. brown sugar

In a 1½-quart casserole, combine all ingredients; stir. Cover and microwave 4 minutes. Let stand 4 minutes, covered. Remove spices and cool. Serves 4 to 6.

BROWN SUGAR BANANAS High

4 medium-ripe bananas
½ c. brown sugar, packed
½ c. golden rum
¼ c. butter
2 T. lime juice
¼ t. nutmeg
¼ c. shredded coconut

Cut bananas in half lengthwise, then in half crosswise. Place in a single layer in an 11 x 7-inch dish. Mix brown sugar, rum, butter, lime juice and nutmeg in a 2-cup measure. Microwave, uncovered, 2½ minutes, stirring after 1 minute. Spoon over bananas. Microwave bananas, uncovered, 2 minutes. Rearrange bananas, moving those in the middle to the outside of the dish, and outside bananas to the middle. Spoon sauce over. Microwave, uncovered, 3 minutes. Sprinkle with coconut. Serves 5 to 6.

Soup and Sauces

When preparing soup, use a bowl twice as large as the amount of ingredients so they will not boil over. If the soup contains raw vegetables, uncooked meat or poultry, microwave on high. For soups containing seafood, cream or buttermilk, use medium cycle. Cover all soups; if using plastic wrap, pierce the top to allow steam to escape. Stir soup when it begins to boil and after half the cooking time has elapsed. Soup will heat through and flavors will mellow during standing time.

To save dishwashing when preparing canned soup, divide the soup into individual serving bowls, dilute and heat, stirring occasionally as it boils.

Sauces take about three to five minutes and should be stirred every minute unless they have been mixed in a blender. In that case, the blender has so thoroughly combined the ingredients that stirring may be eliminated.

BARBECUE SAUCE

1 c. chopped onion
½ c. chopped celery
¼ c. chopped green pepper
3 T. butter
1 clove garlic, minced
1 16-oz. can tomato sauce
2 T. lemon juice
1 T. Worcestershire sauce
1 T. parsley
2 t. sugar
½ t. salt
Few dashes Tabasco sauce

In a 1-quart casserole, combine onion, celery, green pepper, butter and garlic. Cover and microwave 4 minutes, stirring after 2 minutes. Stir in remaining ingredients. Microwave, uncovered, 3 to 4 minutes. Stir after 1½ minutes. Makes 2½ to 3 cups.

CLAM CHOWDER

2 slices bacon
1 7-oz. can minced clams with liquid
1 large potato, peeled and cubed
¼ c. minced onion
½ c. water
1 13-oz. can evaporated milk
Salt and pepper to taste
1 T. butter

Put bacon in a 2-quart casserole. Cover with paper towel. Microwave 1½ to 2 minutes until crisp. Remove paper towel and bacon; leave drippings in casserole. Crumble bacon and set aside. Add clams, liquid, potato, onion and water. Cover and microwave 8 minutes, stirring every 3 minutes. Add milk, bacon, seasonings and butter. Cover and cook 2 to 3 minutes until it comes to a boil. Let stand 2 minutes. Serves 3 to 4.

DESSERT SAUCE /HIGH\

1 3-oz. pkg. regular lemon pudding mix
½ c. sugar
1 t. lemon peel
¼ t. nutmeg
1¼ c. water
1 c. milk
¼ c. brandy

In a 4-cup glass measure, stir together pudding mix, sugar, lemon peel and nutmeg. Gradually stir in water, then milk. Microwave 2 minutes; mixture will appear curdled. Stir, then microwave 3½ minutes more, stirring well after each minute. Mix in brandy. Serve over pound cake, fruit or angel food cake. Makes about 4 servings.

DILL SAUCE /HIGH\

2 T. butter
¼ c. chopped onion
1 10½-oz. can cream of chicken soup
⅔ c. milk
¼ t. dried dill
Dash pepper

Place butter and onion in a 4-cup measure. Cover with waxed paper and microwave 2 minutes, stirring after 1 minute. Add soup, milk, dill and pepper, stirring to blend. Serve hot over vegetables. To warm sauce, heat 1 minute; stir after 30 seconds. Makes 1 cup.

MUSHROOM SAUCE /HIGH\

¼ c. butter
1 2½-oz. jar sliced mushrooms, drained
1 c. light cream
¼ t. salt
2 t. cornstarch

Microwave butter in a 2-cup measure for 45 seconds to melt. Mix in remaining ingredients, stirring smooth. Microwave, uncovered, 2 minutes, stirring after 1 minute. Stir. Cook 2 to 3 minutes until thick. Stir after 1 minute. Serve hot. Makes 1½ cups.

TARRAGON SAUCE /HIGH\

½ c. butter
¼ c. rosé wine
1 T. tarragon vinegar
1 T. snipped chives
½ t. salt
¼ t. pepper
3 egg yolks, slightly beaten

Microwave butter in a small bowl for 45 seconds to melt. Stir in remaining ingredients. Microwave 1 minute, stirring every 15 seconds. Beat until light. Serve cold. Makes 1 cup.

TANGY RHUBARB SAUCE /HIGH\

4 c. sliced rhubarb   ¼ t. nutmeg
2 T. cornstarch   1 c. sugar
1 t. orange peel   ½ c. orange juice

Combine all ingredients in a 1½-quart casserole, stirring well. Cover and microwave 8 minutes. Stir after 4 minutes. Let stand, covered, 5 minutes. Serve hot or cold. Serves 4.

VEGETABLE AND FISH SAUCE /HIGH\

2 c. sliced fresh mushrooms
¼ c. sliced fresh green onion
1 T. flour
¼ t. salt
1 T. butter
⅓ c. milk
1 T. prepared mustard
¼ c. sour cream
2 T. dry white wine

In a 1-quart casserole combine mushrooms and onion; sprinkle with flour and salt. Toss, add butter. Cover and microwave 3½ minutes. Stir well after 1½ minutes. Stir in milk and mustard. Microwave, uncovered, 3 to 4 minutes, stirring every 30 seconds. Stir together wine and sour cream. Add to mushrooms; microwave 30 seconds. Makes 2½ cups.

CHINESE BROWN SAUCE /HIGH

1 T. butter	½ c. water
2 t. cornstarch	4 t. soy sauce
1 t. sugar	

In a 2-cup measure, microwave butter 15 to 30 seconds. Blend in cornstarch and sugar. Add water and soy sauce. Microwave 1½ minutes, stirring twice. Serve hot. Makes ¾ cup.

THICK HAMBURGER SOUP /HIGH

1 lb. ground chuck
2 qts. water
3 bouillon cubes
3 onions, sliced
3 carrots, sliced
1 1-lb. can chopped tomatoes
3 stalks celery, chopped
1 T. salt
1 t. monosodium glutamate
¼ c. quick-cooking rice
½ c. quick-cooking barley

Place meat in a 4-quart casserole. Microwave 5 minutes, stirring twice. Add remaining ingredients and cover. Microwave 45 minutes; stir every 15 minutes. Let stand, covered, 30 minutes before serving. Serves 6 to 8.

CHICKEN SOUP /HIGH

1 3-lb. stewing chicken
4 c. water
½ c. finely chopped onion
½ c. finely chopped celery
2 c. thinly sliced carrot
1 T. salt
½ t. pepper
¼ t. thyme
¼ t. sage
⅓ c. parsley

Combine all ingredients in a 3-quart casserole. Cover and microwave on high for 15 minutes, stirring after 7 minutes. Cook on low 25 to 30 minutes. Remove chicken; cool. Cut meat from bones and cut into small pieces. Return meat to stock. Cover and microwave on low 5 minutes. Let stand, covered, 5 minutes. Serves 6 to 8.

CARROT SOUP /HIGH

4 slices bacon
1 1-lb. can sliced carrots
1 T. grated onion
¼ c. finely diced celery
2 c. chicken broth

Microwave bacon between layers of paper towels for 3½ to 4 minutes. Crumble bacon and set aside. Place carrots and liquid in a 2-quart bowl. Add remaining ingredients and stir. Cover and microwave 3½ minutes. Stir in crumbled bacon. Serves 5.

CHILI /HIGH

1 lb. ground round
1 t. salt
1 pkg. chili seasoning mix
1 1-lb. can kidney beans
1 1-lb. can chopped tomatoes

Place meat in a 2-quart dish. Microwave 3 to 4 minutes, stirring after 2 minutes. Add remaining ingredients, stirring well. Cover and microwave 4 to 6 minutes, stirring after 2 to 2½ minutes. Serves 4.

VEGETABLE SOUP /HIGH

3 slices raw bacon, diced
¼ c. chopped onion
1 c. chopped celery
1 c. thinly sliced carrot
1 c. potatoes, in ¼-inch cubes
3 T. flour
3 c. tomato juice
1 c. water
½ t. thyme
1 cube beef bouillon, crumbled
  Salt and pepper
1 8-oz. can peas and carrots

Place onion and bacon in 2½-quart bowl. Cover and microwave 3 minutes, stirring twice. Add celery, carrots and potatoes. Cover and microwave 10 minutes, stirring twice. Add flour, tomato juice, water, thyme, bouillon, salt and pepper. Heat, uncovered, 10 minutes. Add peas and carrots; heat 3 minutes. Let stand 3 minutes. Serves 6.

18

Pictured opposite
Vegetable soup

CORN AND FRANK CHOWDER

3 slices bacon, chopped
5 wieners, sliced
1 onion, chopped
4 potatoes, diced
1 c. water
2 t. salt
¼ t. pepper
½ t. basil
1 can creamed corn
1 5-oz. can evaporated milk

In a 2½-quart dish, microwave bacon 2½ minutes. Add wieners and onion; microwave 4 minutes, stirring after 2 minutes. Add potatoes and water. Microwave 12 minutes; stir after 6 minutes. Add remaining ingredients and microwave 4 minutes. Serves 4 to 6.

> Place 10 sprigs of parsley or any other herb between sheets of paper toweling. Microwave 3 to 4 minutes. Cool and crumble.
>   Cut ¼ cup chives into ⅛-inch pieces. Place between paper towels. Microwave 2 to 2½ minutes.

CREAM OF ASPARAGUS SOUP

1½ lbs. asparagus
1 onion, finely chopped
1 carrot, thinly sliced
2 stalks celery with leaves,
  thinly sliced
2 potatoes, peeled and chopped
1 t. salt
1 t. seasoned salt
3 c. canned chicken broth
1 c. light cream
½ c. thinly sliced boiled ham,
  cut in small pieces

Cut clean asparagus stalks into 1-inch pieces. Place asparagus, onion, carrot, celery, potatoes, salt and broth in a 2-quart glass bowl. Cover and microwave on high for 11 to 15 minutes until vegetables are tender. Let stand, covered, 5 minutes. Puree soup in a blender. Add cream and ham. Heat on high 5 more minutes. Serves 6 to 8.

TURKEY SOUP WITH DUMPLINGS

1 cooked turkey carcass
2 stalks celery
1 small onion
1 t. salt
½ t. peppercorns
  Pinch mixed herbs
1 c. cooked turkey, cubed

Break up carcass; place in a 4-quart casserole. Add remaining ingredients, except turkey. Add water to halfway up casserole. Microwave 45 minutes; turn dish one-half turn after 23 minutes. Strain. Microwave broth about 4 minutes or until it boils. Add turkey; heat 1 minute. Drop Dumplings by rounded teaspoons into boiling soup. Do not cover. Microwave 2 to 3 minutes on medium cycle until dumplings rise to the top. Serves 6 to 8.

DUMPLINGS

1 egg
¼ c. flour
⅛ t. salt

Combine all ingredients, mixing well.

CORN AND CRAB SOUP

3 T. butter
⅓ c. flour
2 c. milk
2 c. cold water
1 6-oz. can crab meat
1 12-oz. can whole kernel corn
½ t. salt
⅛ t. white pepper
¼ c. light cream

Microwave butter 30 seconds on high to melt. Stir in flour. Gradually stir in milk and water. Microwave 5 minutes until thick, stirring every minute. Drain crab and corn. Remove cartilage from crab. Break crab into small pieces and add with corn, salt and pepper. Cover and microwave on medium speed 5 minutes, stirring after 2½ minutes. Remove from oven and stir in cream. Serves 4 to 6.

Vegetables

The microwave cooks vegetables to perfection—crunchy-crisp yet tender—with all the natural flavor and color. Microwave all vegetables covered. For fresh vegetables, add very little water—a tablespoon or two at the most. Add no water to frozen vegetables. Cook them in the box or pouch in which they came, piercing the top to allow steam to escape.

Bulky or dense vegetables, such as cauliflower, should be broken into smaller pieces for faster cooking. Spread flowerets in a single layer on a cooking platter rather than cooking a whole head.

Stir or rearrange vegetables after half the cooking time to ensure uniform cooking. Season vegetables after they have finished cooking; salt has a tendency to make vegetables tough in the microwave oven.

The American favorite, baked potatoes, are especially good when microwaved. Wash and dry the potatoes early in the day. Roll each potato in a paper napkin which absorbs excess moisture, thus insuring a crisper shell. Microwave a single 8-ounce potato 4½ minutes, 2 potatoes 6 minutes, 3 potatoes 8 minutes and microwave 4 potatoes for 10 minutes.

ORANGE-ALMOND RICE RING /HIGH\

1½ c. long-grain rice
1 c. orange juice
2 c. water
1¼ t. salt
   Whole unblanched almonds

Combine rice, orange juice, water and salt in a 2-quart casserole. Cover and microwave 7 to 8 minutes, stirring after 3½ minutes. Let stand 10 minutes, still covered. Microwave, covered, 4 to 5 minutes. Butter a 5-cup fluted ring mold. Arrange almonds in bottom; spoon rice over, packing lightly. Microwave 3 to 5 minutes, uncovered. Invert onto serving plate. Serves 6 to 8.

CRUNCHY CRUSTED POTATOES /HIGH\

2 potatoes, peeled and quartered
¼ c. butter
½ c. cornflake crumbs
¼ t. salt
⅛ t. pepper
¼ t. paprika

Place butter in a custard cup and microwave 30 to 45 seconds. Set aside. Mix cornflake crumbs, salt, pepper and paprika in a bowl. Dip each potato piece into butter, then into the crumb mixture. Arrange in a circle on a large platter. Cover with a paper towel and microwave 6 minutes. Turn dish one-half turn after 3 minutes. Serves 2 or 3.

CAULIFLOWER AU GRATIN High

1 pkg. frozen cauliflower
2 T. water
¼ c. herb-seasoned stuffing mix
½ c. shredded Cheddar cheese

Place cauliflower and water in a 1½-quart casserole. Cover and microwave 8 to 9 minutes, stirring after 4 minutes. Drain liquid and reserve. Combine stuffing, liquid and cheese. Sprinkle over the cauliflower. Cover and microwave 1 to 2 minutes. Serves 3 to 4.

To blanch vegetables for freezing, wash vegetables and place in a 2-quart casserole. Add ¼ cup water. Do not salt. Cover and microwave 3¼ minutes per pound of vegetable, rearranging after half the cooking time. Plunge vegetables into cold water; blot with paper toweling and freeze.

SCALLOPED POTATOES High

4 medium potatoes, pared and thinly sliced
3 T. flour
¾ t. salt
1 c. milk, scalded
2 T. butter
Paprika

Arrange half of the potatoes in a 1½-quart casserole. Combine flour and salt; sprinkle half over the potatoes. Layer remaining potatoes and flour and salt. Pour milk over; dot with butter and sprinkle with paprika. Cover and microwave 11 to 12 minutes. Turn dish after 5½ minutes. Stand, covered, 5 minutes. Serve hot. Serves 4 to 6.

HARVARD BEETS High

1 16-oz. can sliced beets, undrained
1 T. cornstarch
1 T. plus 1 t. sugar
¾ t. salt
¼ c. vinegar

Drain liquid from beets into a measuring cup. Add enough water to make ⅔ cup. Set aside. In a deep 1½-quart casserole, mix cornstarch, sugar and salt. Gradually add beet liquid and vinegar; stirring smooth. Microwave, covered, 1½ minutes. Stir. Microwave 1 minute, stirring after 30 seconds. Add beets; heat, uncovered, 3 minutes. Serves 4.

GOURMET VEGETABLE SUPREME High

1 16-oz. bag mixed frozen vegetables
1 can water chestnuts, sliced
1 10½-oz. can cream of celery soup
1 can French-fried onion rings

Place frozen vegetables in a 2½-quart casserole. Cover with plastic wrap and microwave 8 minutes, turning dish one-quarter turn after 4 minutes. Uncover; spread water chestnuts on top of vegetables. Spread the undiluted soup over chestnuts. Top with onion rings. Heat, uncovered, 4 minutes. Serves 6 to 8.

VEGETABLE CREPES High

1 10-oz. pkg. frozen broccoli
1 T. water
Salt and pepper to taste
6 frozen crepes

Place frozen broccoli in a 1½-quart casserole. Add water. Microwave, covered, 8 to 9 minutes, stirring after 4 minutes. Set aside. Place one or two stalks of broccoli on each crepe; roll up. Place 3 crepes on a plate and microwave 1 to 1½ minutes. Drizzle with Cheese Sauce. Serves 4 to 6.

CHEESE SAUCE / Med

1 10½-oz. can Cheddar cheese soup
2 T. water

Blend soup and water in a 2-cup measuring cup. Microwave 3 minutes on medium. Stir after 1½ minutes.

Pictured opposite
Vegetable Crepes

CHEESY CRUMB TOMATOES

4 tomatoes
⅓ c. bread crumbs
   Dash pepper
½ t. salt
2 T. grated Parmesan cheese
2 T. butter

Cut tomatoes in half crosswise and arrange on serving plate, cut side up. In a small bowl, combine bread crumbs, salt, pepper, Parmesan cheese and butter. Microwave, uncovered, 3 to 4 minutes until brown, stirring frequently. Sprinkle crumb mixture over tomatoes. Microwave, uncovered, 3 to 4 minutes, turning a half turn after 2 minutes. Serves 4.

SWEET POTATOES IN ORANGES

3 oranges, halved
1 2½-lb. can sweet potatoes
3 T. melted butter
¼ c. brown sugar
1 t. salt
1 t. cinnamon
2 T. brown sugar

Remove pulp from oranges. Chop pulp fine and reserve. Drain potatoes and mash. Combine potatoes, orange pulp, butter, salt and ¼ cup brown sugar; mix. Spoon into empty orange shells. Combine cinnamon and 2 tablespoons brown sugar. Sprinkle 1 teaspoon over each orange shell. Place in a circle on a large glass plate; microwave 8 minutes. Turn plate one-half turn after 4 minutes. Serves 6.

> To prevent a last-minute rush, partially cook some foods before mealtime. Later, pop them in the oven to finish cooking.

SPINACH SOUFFLE

¼ c. butter
¼ c. flour
1 t. salt
⅛ t. pepper
¼ t. dry mustard
1 c. milk
1 10-oz. pkg. frozen spinach, defrosted and drained
4 eggs, separated
1 t. cream of tartar

Place butter in a 1½-quart casserole; microwave 30 seconds. Stir in flour, salt, pepper and dry mustard, making a smooth paste. Gradually stir in milk, mixing well. Microwave 3 to 4 minutes, stirring twice. Add spinach and slightly beaten egg yolks. In a large bowl, beat egg whites with cream of tartar until stiff. Gently fold mustard sauce into egg whites. Pour into a 6 to 8-cup soufflé dish. Microwave on medium 2 minutes and on low for 25 to 30 minutes. Serves 6 to 8.

SHERRIED SWEET POTATOES

6 medium-size sweet potatoes
4 T. butter
½ c. brown sugar
⅔ c. orange juice
½ t. grated orange peel
⅓ c. sherry
1 c. coarsely chopped pecans

Rinse and dry potatoes. Pierce with a fork. Place on a layer of paper towels. Microwave 10 to 12 minutes. Turn towels one-half turn after 3 minutes and again after 6 minutes. Peel and cut in 1-inch slices. Place butter in a 10-inch skillet; heat 30 seconds. Add potatoes. Microwave 1 minute; stir and heat 1 additional minute. Combine remaining ingredients and pour over potatoes. Mix gently. Cover and microwave 5 to 6 minutes, turning dish after half cooking time has passed. Serves 4 to 6.

CANDIED CARROTS HIGH

4 large carrots	1 t. salt
⅓ c. butter	⅓ t. cinnamon
½ c. sugar	1 T. water

Scrape carrots and cut into thin strips. Place in a deep 1½-quart casserole; set aside. In a small bowl, combine remaining ingredients. Heat 1 minute; spoon sauce over carrots. Cover and microwave 3½ minutes. Stir and baste with sauce. Microwave an additional 3½ minutes. Heat, uncovered, 3 minutes. Serves 3 to 4.

MASHED POTATOES HIGH

4 large red potatoes	1½ t. salt
	¾ c. milk
¼ c. water	2 T. butter

Peel potatoes and cut into eighths. Place potatoes and water in a 2-quart bowl. Cover with plastic wrap or a glass cover. Microwave 10 to 14 minutes, turning dish a half turn after 6 minutes. Let stand, covered, 5 minutes. Drain. Whip potatoes with remaining ingredients. Serves 6.

SPANISH RICE HIGH

4 slices bacon
1 1-lb. can tomatoes
¾ c. water
1 box Spanish rice mix

Place bacon on the bacon grid and cover with paper towel. Microwave 2½ to 3 minutes. Reserve 2 tablespoons of the drippings. Combine tomatoes, water, reserved drippings and Spanish rice mix. Stir. Cover and microwave 8 minutes; stir after 4 minutes. Let stand, covered, 5 minutes. Crumble bacon on top for garnish. Serves 4 to 6.

CORN RELISH HIGH

1 c. sugar
2 T. cornstarch
2 T. minced onion
1 T. mustard seed
¼ t. celery seed
¼ t. turmeric
1 c. vinegar
¾ c. hot water
½ c. pimiento, minced
3 12-oz. cans whole kernel corn, drained

In a 3-quart casserole, combine first 6 ingredients. Gradually add vinegar and water, stirring well. Cover and microwave 5 minutes; stir well. Add corn and pimiento. Cover; microwave 15 to 17 minutes, stirring after 7 minutes. Stir when finished cooking. Makes 1½ to 2 cups.

> When cooking different sizes of similar items, put the larger items in the oven first. Add smaller items a minute or two later, so they will all finish cooking at the same time.

PIZZA POTATOES HIGH

1 box scalloped potatoes
1 16-oz. can tomatoes
1½ c. boiling water
¼ t. oregano
1 4-oz. pkg. sliced pepperoni
1 4-oz. pkg. shredded mozzarella cheese

Empty potato slices into a 3-quart round casserole. Stir in sauce mix, tomatoes, water and oregano. Cover and microwave 10 minutes, stirring twice during cooking. Stir in pepperoni; sprinkle with cheese. Cover and microwave 7 minutes, stirring after 3½ minutes. Uncover and let stand 5 minutes before serving. Serves 4 to 6.

Meats and Main Dishes

When cooking meats, popping sounds are often heard; this is only from the activity of the fat and nothing to be concerned about. Less tender cuts of meat, such as beef stew meat, chuck roast, Swiss steak or corned beef become tender if cooked on low cycle. Other meats are microwaved on high, such as prime rib, steak, or hamburger. If a well-done roast is desired, cut the roast in half and turn the ends to the middle after half the cooking time. A roast or fowl over three pounds will brown naturally, but for a browned roast under three pounds, brush with Kitchen Bouquet or use a glaze or sauce. Do not salt meat before cooking.

Cover meat, poultry and fish with waxed paper to keep them moist and juicy; cover steaks with a paper towel to absorb the fat. When stewing chicken, cover it with plastic wrap before microwaving. For a crispy crust, coat poultry with crumbs and place on a rack. Microwave, uncovered, turning dish one-half turn after half the cooking time has elapsed.

Poultry requires special care in a microwave oven. Shield the thin parts of wings and legs by wrapping those portions with foil during either the first or last half of the cooking time. Arrange pieces with the thicker portions of the meat toward the outside of the dish.

The following meat timing chart shows the minutes-per-pound cooking time for various meats. After the meat is taken from the oven, it will continue cooking. The Temperature after Standing refers to the final internal temperature of the meat.

MEAT TIMING CHART		
	Minutes Per Pound	Temperature After Standing
Beef		
Rare	5½	140°
Medium	6½	160°
Well-done	7½-8	170°
Veal		
Medium	8-8½	170°
Well-done	9-9½	170°
Pork		
Fresh, well-done	10	170°
Pre-cooked	5	150°
Lamb	9-9½	180°
Fish	4-5	170°
Poultry	7	190°

Pictured opposite
Italian French Bread Special
(page 29)

BEEF JERKY

3 lbs. flank steak, trim excess fat
1 T. salt
1 t. garlic salt
½ t. pepper

Freeze steak partially to ease in slicing. Mix spices together and set aside. Cut steak lengthwise with the grain into ⅛-inch slices. Place 4 to 6 slices meat on bacon grid. Sprinkle with spice mixture. Cover with paper towel. Microwave 2 to 3 minutes. Turn meat over. Sprinkle with spices. Cover with towel. Microwave 2 to 3 minutes. Dry on paper towel. Repeat, using all the meat. Makes 3 pounds jerky.

ALL-IN-ONE FAMILY CASSEROLE

1½ lbs. ground round
1 1-lb. can French-style green beans
1 1-lb. can shoestring carrots
1 10-oz. can cream of celery soup
½ can milk
1 3-oz. can chow mein noodles

Microwave ground round in a 2-quart casserole for 4 to 5 minutes, stirring after 2 minutes to break up meat. Drain vegetables; mix soup with milk. Layer beans, carrots and soup on top of meat and cover with plastic wrap. Microwave 5 minutes, turning one-half turn after 2½ minutes. Top with noodles. Heat 1 minute, uncovered. Makes 4 to 6 servings.

SUMMER SAUSAGE

3 lbs. ground round
1½ t. cracked peppercorns
1½ t. mustard seed
¾ t. garlic salt
¾ t. onion salt
1 T. curing salt
1½ t. liquid smoke

Combine all ingredients in a large bowl. Knead with hands. Cover with plastic wrap and refrigerate for 24 hours. Divide into 3 parts. Shape each part into a 12-inch roll. Place the 3 rolls on a roasting rack. Cover with paper towels. Microwave on low or at 30 percent power for 20 minutes. Turn rolls over and rearrange. Microwave at low or 30 percent power for an additional 20 to 25 minutes (until internal temperature is 140°). Cool and wrap tightly. Refrigerate. Slice to serve. Makes 3 servings.

NOTE: These can be made with higher power. Microwave 5 minutes, let stand 10 minutes. Turn sausages and rearrange. Repeat 2 more times.

MEATBALLS ITALIAN

1 lb. ground round
1 c. quick-cooking rice
1 10-oz. can condensed tomato-rice soup
1 egg
½ c. water
1 t. Nature's Seasoning

Mix beef, rice, ½ can soup, egg, water and seasoning. Shape into 12 balls. Place in a circle in a 10-inch pie plate. Cover with waxed paper. Microwave 6 to 7 minutes, turning disc one-half turn after 3 minutes. Spoon Topping over meatballs. Cover and microwave 2 to 4 minutes. Serves 4.

TOPPING

½ can tomato-rice soup
2 T. spaghetti sauce
1 t. dry mustard

Combine all ingredients and mix well.

ITALIAN FRENCH BREAD SPECIAL

French bread
1 6-oz. can tomato paste
¼ c. water
⅓ c. grated Parmesan cheese
¼ c. chopped onion
½ c. chopped ripe olives
½ t. oregano
½ t. fennel
¾ t. salt
⅛ t. pepper
1 lb. ground chuck
4 tomatoes, sliced
1 8-oz. pkg. American cheese

Combine tomato paste, water, Parmesan, onion, olives and seasonings. Preheat browning skillet 4½ minutes. Crumble ground chuck into skillet. Microwave 4 minutes, stirring after 2 minutes. Drain grease. Add tomato mixture. Slice French bread in half lengthwise. Spread mixture over both halves of bread and top with tomato slices. Cover with waxed paper and microwave 2 minutes. Garnish with cheese cut into strips. Microwave 1½ to 2 minutes, melting cheese. Serves 8.

TACOS

1 lb. ground round
1 pkg. taco seasoning mix
½ c. water
10 taco shells
Shredded lettuce
Shredded Cheddar cheese
Chopped fresh tomato

Crumble beef in a 1-quart casserole. Sprinkle with taco mix. Microwave 5 minutes, stirring twice. Add water and cover with a paper towel. Microwave 3 to 5 minutes. Spoon into taco shells and place in a 12 x 8-inch dish. Microwave 1½ minutes. Serve with lettuce, cheese and tomato. Makes 10 tacos.

CHINESE BURGERS

1 lb. ground chuck
¼ c. chopped onion
1 T. prepared mustard
2 T. tomato sauce
2 T. soy sauce
½ t. garlic powder
¼ t. pepper
1 t. prepared horseradish
1½ c. bean sprouts, drained and rinsed
½ c. sour cream
8 hamburger buns

Place ground chuck and onion in a 1½-quart casserole; cover. Microwave 2½ minutes; stir. Cover; microwave 2½ minutes. Pour off grease and stir in mustard, tomato sauce, soy sauce, garlic powder, pepper, horseradish and bean sprouts. Microwave 2 minutes. Stir in sour cream. Microwave 30 seconds. Spoon on buns. Serves 4.

MEAT LOAF

1½ lb. ground round
1 slice bread, crumbled
1 egg
1 stalk celery
1 small onion
2 T. water
2 T. catsup
2 T. brown sugar

Add bread crumbs to meat; mix well. Combine egg, celery, onion and water in a blender. Blend to smooth. Add to meat and mix well. Place in a loaf pan; score top. Mix together catsup and brown sugar. Pour over top of meat and microwave 6 minutes, turning dish one-half turn after 3 minutes. Turn pan one-half turn and shield with foil. Microwave an additional 6 minutes, turning dish one-half turn after 3 minutes. Let stand, covered, 5 minutes. Serves 4 to 5.

ENCHILADAS

1 medium onion, chopped
1 T. water
1 lb. ground round
½ c. shredded Cheddar cheese
½ c. sour cream
2 t. parsley flakes
1 t. seasoned salt
⅛ t. pepper
10 to 12 flour tortillas
1 15-oz. can tomato sauce
½ c. chopped green pepper
2 t. chili powder
½ t. oregano
⅛ t. minced garlic
½ c. water

Combine onion and water in a 1½-quart covered casserole and microwave 2 to 3 minutes. Add crumbled ground round. Microwave 2½ minutes; stir and microwave an additional 2½ minutes. Drain. Add cheese, sour cream, parsley flakes, salt and pepper. Set aside. Wrap tortillas in paper toweling and microwave 1 minute. Combine remaining ingredients. Pour half of this sauce mixture into a 12 x 8-inch dish. Place 2½ tablespoons meat mixture in center of each tortilla. Roll up. Place seam side down in the sauce. Top with remaining sauce. Cover with plastic wrap. Heat 11 to 12 minutes. Turn after 5½ to 6 minutes. Serves 6 to 8.

SATURDAY NIGHT CASSEROLE

½ c. chopped onion
1 lb. ground chuck
1 can drained whole kernel corn
1 8-oz. pkg. softened cream cheese
1 10½-oz. can cream of mushroom soup
1 2-oz. jar chopped pimiento
1 t. salt

In a 2-quart casserole, combine onion and ground chuck. Microwave 2½ minutes; stir and microwave an additional 2½ minutes. In a separate bowl, combine remaining ingredients, mixing well. Add to meat and onion, stirring to blend. Cover and microwave 8 minutes. Serves 6 to 8.

POT ROAST

1 3-lb. beef roast
¼ c. creamy horseradish
¾ c. Burgundy
½ pkg. dry onion soup mix
2 bay leaves
6 whole allspice
Beau Monde
Mei Yen
Salt
Pepper

Preheat browning skillet 4½ minutes. Place roast in skillet and microwave 1 minute. Turn and microwave other side 1 minute. Spread top and sides of roast with horseradish. Warm Burgundy and add dry onion soup mix. Slowly pour this mixture over the roast, being careful not to wash off the horseradish. Add bay leaves, allspice and sprinkle with salt and pepper, Mei Yen and Beau Monde. Cover. Microwave on medium cycle 90 minutes. Turn roast after 35 minutes. Turn dish one-quarter turn every 20 minutes. Serves 4 to 6.

> Dense items such as roasts and poultry over three pounds should be completely turned over after half the cooking time for uniform cooking.

STUFFED GREEN PEPPERS

3 medium green peppers
¾ lb. ground round
⅓ c. quick cooking rice
1 t. salt
¼ t. pepper
1 egg
⅓ c. water
1 c. tomato sauce

Cut green peppers in half, lengthwise; remove core and seeds. Place peppers in a 12 x 8-inch dish. Combine remaining ingredients, using only ½ cup of tomato sauce. Spoon mixture into pepper halves. Spoon remaining tomato sauce over the meat. Cover with waxed paper and microwave, 10 to 12 minutes, turning dish one-half turn after 5 minutes. Let stand, covered, 5 minutes. Serves 4 to 6.

Pictured opposite
Enchiladas

GOURMET BEEF STEW MED

¾ lb. beef stew meat
1 T. flour
½ t. salt
1 T. shortening
1 6-oz. can tomato sauce
  Clove garlic, minced
1 bay leaf
  Dash thyme
½ t. monosodium glutamate
¾ c. dry red wine, consomme or water
2 t. vinegar
2 carrots, peeled and sliced
1 potato, diced
1 celery stalk, sliced
2 onions, peeled and cut into eighths
½ c. frozen green peas

Coat meat with mixture of flour and salt. Preheat browning skillet for 4½ minutes. Add shortening. Add meat and brown on all sides for 1 minute. Add tomato sauce, seasonings, wine and vinegar. Set oven to medium or to automatic defrost cycle. Cover and cook 50 minutes, stirring 2 times. Add potato, carrots, celery and onions; and microwave for 9 minutes. Add peas; microwave 1 minute. Serves 4.

SWISS STEAK  HIGH / MED

2 lbs. round steak
1 envelope onion soup mix
1 green pepper, sliced
1 1-lb. can tomatoes, drained
½ c. tomato juice
1 T. flour

Cut steak into serving-size pieces. Preheat browning skillet 4½ minutes. Place meat in skillet and microwave 1 minute on each side. Sprinkle with soup mix. Add pepper slices and tomatoes. Heat tomato juice; stir in flour and pour over steak. Cover. Microwave on medium cycle 50 to 55 minutes, turning dish one-quarter turn every 20 minutes. Serves 4 to 6.

BEEF ROLL-UPS HIGH

8 slices bacon
8 pieces top round, thinly sliced
1 medium onion, thinly sliced
⅓ c. flour
1 T. beef bouillon
½ t. salt
⅛ t. pepper
1½ c. water
½ c. dry red wine

On paper plate, layer bacon between toweling. Microwave 4 to 5 minutes. Place slice of bacon on each piece of meat. Divide onion slices among meat slices. Roll up each slice and fasten with a toothpick. Coat with flour. Preheat browning skillet 4½ minutes; add bacon drippings. Brown meat 1 minute on each side. Add remaining flour and ingredients; mix lightly. Cover. Microwave 10 minutes, turning dish one-half turn after 3 minutes and again after 6 minutes. Let stand 10 minutes. Microwave another 6 to 8 minutes, turning dish one-quarter turn after 5 minutes of cooking time. Serves 4.

MEATBALLS HIGH

1 lb. ground round
1 slice bread, crumbled
1 egg
  Salt and pepper to taste

Mix meat, bread crumbs, egg and seasonings together; form into walnut-size balls. Place meatballs around the edge of an 8-inch round dish and cover with waxed paper. Microwave 4 to 5 minutes until done. Cover with Sauce. Microwave, 3 to 4 minutes. Turn dish one-quarter turn every 3 minutes. Serves 3 to 4.

SAUCE

1 15-oz. can tomato sauce
½ c. water
⅓ c. Parmesan cheese
⅛ t. pepper
2 T. diced onion
2 T. diced celery

Mix together all ingredients, blending well.

SEAFOOD GARDEN HIGH

2 pkgs. frozen asparagus
¼ c. water
1 3-oz. pkg. cream cheese, softened
1 10½-oz. can cream of shrimp soup
2 dashes cayenne
1 can small shrimp, drained
2 T. melted butter
½ c. cracker crumbs
   Paprika

Combine asparagus with water in a 1½-quart casserole; microwave 10 minutes. Turn dish and separate pieces after 5 minutes. Drain and set aside. Combine cream cheese, soup and cayenne; beat until smooth. Stir in shrimp. Pour over asparagus. Mix melted butter and cracker crumbs, stirring thoroughly. Sprinkle buttered crumbs and paprika on top of asparagus. Microwave 8 to 10 minutes. After 5 minutes, turn dish one-half turn. Serves 6.

ORANGE SOY FILLETS HIGH

2 T. soy sauce
2 T. frozen orange concentrate, thawed
1 T. lemon juice
1 T. catsup
1 clove garlic, minced
1 lb. frozen fish fillets, thawed

Combine soy sauce, orange and lemon juices, catsup and garlic in a 12 x 7-inch dish. Place fillets in mixture, arranging with thick edges to the outside of the dish. Cover with plastic wrap. Microwave 6 to 8 minutes. Let stand, covered, 5 minutes. Serves 2 to 3.

LOW-CALORIE FISH HIGH

1 lb. fish fillets   ⅛ t. pepper
2 T. lemon juice   ⅛ t. paprika
¼ c. water   ¼ t. parsley
1 t. salt

Place a 10 x 16-inch browning bag in a 10 x 6-inch dish. Place fish in a single layer in the bag. Combine remaining ingredients in a bowl. Pour over fish. Close bag with a rubber band. Make six ½-inch slits in the top of bag. Microwave 4 to 5 minutes, turning dish after 2 minutes. Serve with Cucumber Sauce. Serves 2 to 3.

CUCUMBER SAUCE

¾ c. diced and peeled cucumber
1 T. grated lemon rind
2 sliced green onions
½ c. mayonnaise
¼ t. dill weed

Combine all ingredients, blending well.

FRENCH FISH FILLETS HIGH

1 lb. fish
¼ c. French dressing
½ c. cracker crumbs
   Paprika

Dip fish in French dressing then in crumbs. Place in a greased, shallow baking dish. Sprinkle with paprika and cover with waxed paper. Microwave 4 to 6 minutes, turning dish after 2½ minutes. Serves 2 to 3.

CRAB NEWBURG HIGH

¼ c. butter   ¼ c. sherry
1½ T. flour   2 c. flaked crab
½ t. salt   meat
1½ c. light cream   1 t. lemon juice
2 egg yolks

Place butter in a 1½-quart casserole; microwave 30 seconds to melt. Stir in flour and salt, blending well. Beat cream with egg yolks and add to butter mixture. Stir in sherry, blending until smooth. Add crab; cover and microwave 7 minutes, stirring occasionally. Add lemon juice; serve over rice. Serves 6.

CLAM NOODLE CASSEROLE High

2 T. butter
1 green onion, chopped
2 T. flour
1 t. salt
2 c. milk
1 can minced clams, with juice
1 8-oz. pkg. wide noodles, cooked
½ c. fresh bread crumbs
1 T. grated Parmesan cheese

Place butter in a 2-quart casserole. Microwave 30 seconds to melt. Add onion; microwave 1 minute; stir and microwave 1 minute more. Mix milk, flour and salt. Gradually add to butter mixture. Mix well. Microwave to a thick and very smooth texture and until mixture comes to a boil (about 8 minutes), stirring every minute. Blend in noodles and clams. Top with bread crumbs and cheese. Microwave 5 minutes, uncovered. Makes 4 servings.

FISH FILLETS WITH MUSHROOMS High

3 T. butter
2 green peppers, cut in ½-inch slices
¼ lb. thinly sliced fresh mushrooms
1½ lbs. fish fillets
Shredded peel of 1 lemon
¼ c. sliced water chestnuts, drained
Salt
Pepper
Paprika

Place green peppers and butter in a 12 x 8-inch dish. Cover with plastic wrap and microwave 3 minutes. Stir after 1½ minutes. Add mushrooms; stir and microwave 5 minutes. Stir after 2½ minutes. Add fish, lemon peel and chestnuts. Spoon sauce over fish. Cover with waxed paper, and microwave 5 to 6 minutes. Stir after 3 minutes. Season, if desired, with salt, pepper and paprika. Serve over cooked rice. Serves 4.

SAUCY FILLETS High

1 lb. fish fillets
2 T. fresh lemon juice
¼ c. water
1 t. salt
⅛ t. pepper
⅛ t. paprika
¼ t. parsley flakes

Place fish in a single layer in a 10 x 6-inch dish. Stir remaining ingredients together and pour over fish. Cover with waxed paper. Microwave 4 to 5 minutes, stirring after 2 minutes. Serve with Tangy Sauce. Serves 2 to 3.

TANGY SAUCE

¾ c. diced and peeled cucumber
1 T. grated lemon rind
1 T. sliced onion
½ c. mayonnaise
¼ t. dill weed

Mix together all ingredients. Refrigerate to marinate. Garnish with parsley.

SEAFOOD STUFFED PEPPERS High

2 green peppers
1 10-oz. can mushroom soup
1 7-oz. can tuna, drained and flaked
½ c. shredded Cheddar cheese
½ c. cooked noodles
¼ c. water

Cut peppers in half lengthwise. Remove seeds. Place peppers in a 10 x 6-inch casserole. Cover with waxed paper. Microwave 6 to 8 minutes, turning dish one-quarter turn after 3 minutes. Combine one-half can soup and remaining ingredients except water. Spoon into peppers. Blend remaining soup and water. Pour over peppers and cover with waxed paper. Microwave 8 to 10 minutes, turning dish one-quarter turn every 3 minutes. Serves 3 to 4.

*Pictured opposite
Seafood Garden
(page 33)*

CHICKEN CHOW MEIN

1 lb. chicken breasts
1 10½-oz. can cream of celery soup
½ lb. cashews
1 can sliced water chestnuts, drained
1 3-oz. can chow mein noodles
2 c. diagonally sliced celery
1 green pepper, thinly sliced
1 c. sliced mushrooms

Place chicken in a 7 x 11-inch dish. Cover and microwave 7 minutes. Let stand, still covered, 5 minutes. Cool. Remove meat from bones and cut into bite-size pieces. Combine all ingredients in a 12 x 8-inch casserole along with the broth from the cooked chicken; mix well. Cover and microwave 6 minutes, turning dish one-half turn after 3 minutes. Serves 6 to 8.

POULTRY DELIGHT

1 c. rice
2 c. water
1 pkg. frozen French green beans
   with almonds
1 can cream of celery soup
¼ c. water
1½ c. cut-up cooked chicken
1 can sliced water chestnuts, drained

Place 1 cup rice in a 2-quart mixing bowl. Add 2 cups water. Cover with plastic wrap and microwave 6 minutes. Let stand, covered, 6 minutes. Microwave 6 additional minutes. Let stand, covered, 6 minutes. Fluff up with a fork. Remove almonds from box of beans. Microwave beans 5 to 6 minutes in oven. (Poke a hole in the plastic pouch before microwaving.) Mix together beans, soup, water, poultry and chestnuts. Place in a 2-quart casserole. Microwave 4 to 5 minutes. Serve over rice. Garnish with almonds. Serves 3.

TURKEY LOAF

¼ c. butter
3 T. flour
2 c. milk
2 eggs
1 t. salt
¼ t. pepper
3 c. finely diced cooked turkey
3 c. leftover turkey stuffing
¾ c. wheat germ
2 T. lemon juice

Place butter in a 4-cup measure; microwave 30 seconds to melt. Stir in flour and milk. Mix well. Microwave until smooth and thick, about 8 minutes. After 4 minutes, stir every minute. Cool slightly. Beat eggs slightly. Gradually beat into sauce. Add salt, pepper, turkey, stuffing, wheat germ and lemon juice. Spray a 9 x 5-inch loaf dish very lightly with vegetable spray. Shape turkey mixture into a loaf and place in pan. Cover with waxed paper, microwave 5 minutes, turning one-quarter turn every 2½ minutes. Shield with foil and microwave an additional 5 minutes. Serve with Sauce. Makes 6 to 8 servings.

SAUCE

1 c. mayonnaise
½ c. sour cream
2 T. prepared mustard

Mix well.

ROAST TURKEY

Wash turkey; secure opening with string. Place turkey, breast side *down*, on roasting rack. Melt ½ cup butter; add ¼ teaspoon paprika. Brush with butter. Cover bird with waxed paper and microwave at 7 minutes per pound. Divide total cooking time by 4. After the first quarter of time, turn turkey completely over and brush with butter mixture. Turn dish one-quarter turn and microwave for the second quarter of cooking time. Let turkey stand in oven 10 minutes. Shield wings and legs. Microwave turkey for the two remaining quarters, turning bird over and turning dish one-quarter turn between each quarter. Pour off juices after each quarter of cooking time. Let stand 15 minutes before carving.

CHAMPAGNE CHICKEN

    3 T. butter
    6 mushroom caps
    6 whole chicken breasts, skinned
      and boned
  ¼ c. chicken broth
  ¼ c. champagne
    3 T. melted butter
    3 T. flour
1½ c. light cream
    1 t. black, cracked pepper
  ½ t. salt
  ½ t. dry mustard

Melt 3 tablespoons butter in a 12 x 7-inch dish. Add 6 mushroom caps, turning to coat. Microwave 1 minute, uncovered. Remove and set aside. Add chicken breasts to dish, turning to coat with butter. Arrange chicken in a single layer in a cooking dish. Pour ¼ cup chicken broth and ¼ cup champagne over the chicken. Cover with plastic wrap. Microwave 10 minutes, turning after 5 minutes. Drain pan juice, setting aside ½ cup. Mix melted butter and flour in a 2-quart container. Gradually add 1½ cups light cream. Microwave 2 minutes, stirring every 30 seconds, until thick and smooth. Gradually stir in reserved pan juices and add cracked pepper, salt and mustard. Microwave 2 minutes, stirring after each minute. Pour sauce over chicken; microwave, covered, 5 minutes. Top with reserved mushrooms and serve. Serves 4 to 6.

TURKEY CASSEROLE

    1 c. diced celery
1¼ c. water
  ½ c. melted butter
    1 8-oz. pkg. onion and sage stuffing
    2 c. cooked turkey
    2 10½-oz. cans undiluted cream of
      celery soup

Place celery in baking dish; cover with plastic wrap and microwave 1½ minutes. Let stand, covered, 5 minutes. Combine water, butter and stuffing. In a 12 x 8-inch casserole, layer celery, meat and stuffing. Pour soup over top, spreading evenly. Cover and microwave 8 minutes, turning dish one-half turn after 4 minutes. Serves 6 to 8.

PRIZE-WINNING ELEGANT CHICKEN

    2 10-oz. pkgs. frozen asparagus spears
  ¼ c. butter
  ¼ c. blanched, slivered almonds
  ¼ c. flour
  ½ t. salt
  ⅛ t. pepper
    1 10½-oz. can chicken and rice soup
    1 c. chicken broth
    3 c. cooked chicken, cut bite size
      Paprika

Slit tops of boxes of asparagus. Microwave in boxes 10 minutes. After 5 minutes, open boxes and rearrange asparagus spears. Set aside. Microwave butter in 9-inch pie plate for 30 seconds. Add almonds to butter. Microwave 1½ minutes, stirring every 30 seconds. Mix together flour, salt, pepper and toasted almonds. Add soup and broth, stirring well. Microwave 3 to 5 minutes, stirring every 1 minute, until thick. In a 12 x 8-inch casserole, alternate layers of chicken and asparagus. Cover with butter sauce. Sprinkle with paprika. Cover with plastic wrap and microwave 5 to 6 minutes. Turn dish one-half turn after 2½ minutes. Garnish with almonds and parsley. Serves 6 to 8.

CHICKEN DIVAN

    2 10-oz. pkgs. frozen broccoli spears
  ¾ c. cubed chicken
  ½ c. mayonnaise
    1 10½-oz. cream of chicken soup
    1 T. lemon juice
  ½ c. sour cream
  ½ t. curry
    1 c. shredded Cheddar cheese
  ½ c. cracker crumbs
      Slivered almonds

Place broccoli in a 12 x 7-inch dish; cover with plastic wrap. Microwave 10 minutes; drain. Place chicken on top of broccoli. Blend mayonnaise, chicken soup, lemon juice, sour cream and curry. Stir in cheese. Pour over chicken. Sprinkle with cracker crumbs and top with almonds. Cover and microwave 6 to 7 minutes. Serves 6.

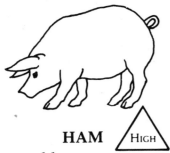

HAM

1 3-lb. canned ham
Whole cloves
½ c. brown sugar
2 t. dry mustard
¼ c. orange marmalade

Place ham in a dish and microwave 5 minutes. Remove from oven and score top. Place cloves in top of ham. Combine remaining ingredients. Spread over ham; microwave 10 minutes. Baste several times. Let stand 10 minutes. Serves 6.

BARBECUED PORK CHOPS

6 pork chops, ½ inch thick
1 c. barbecue sauce
½ c. chopped onion
⅛ t. minced garlic
½ t. salt
⅛ t. pepper

Arrange chops in a 12 x 8-inch dish. Combine remaining ingredients. Pour over the chops. Cover with plastic wrap and microwave 5 minutes. Let stand covered 5 minutes. Repeat 2 more times, basting with sauce during rest times. If need be, chops can be cooked 5 minutes more after the last standing time. Turn the dish one-quarter turn after each rest period. Serves 4.

SAUSAGE CASSEROLE

½ c. bulk pork sausage, broken up
1 medium onion, chopped
½ green pepper, diced
1 16-oz. can pork and beans
1 8-oz. can pineapple chunks, drained
1 t. salt
½ t. dry mustard

Combine meat, onion and green pepper in a 10 x 6-inch dish. Cover with plastic wrap. Microwave 5 minutes, stirring twice to break up meat. Pour off fat. Mix remaining ingredients and pour over meat. Cover and microwave 10 minutes, stirring twice. Serves 3.

SCALLOPED POTATOES AND HAM

7 medium potatoes, sliced
2 T. water
2 c. milk
2 T. butter
2 T. flour
1 t. salt
¼ t. pepper
2 T. chopped onion
2 c. chopped ham
4 slices cooked bacon, crumbled

Place sliced potatoes in a 2-quart casserole and cover. Microwave 12 minutes. Set aside. Microwave milk 1 to 2 minutes or until warm. Set aside. Place butter in a large oven-proof measure; microwave 4 to 5 minutes to melt. Stir in flour, seasonings and warm milk. Arrange ham over potatoes and top with milk mixture. Microwave 5 minutes, garnish with bacon. Serves 6.

HAM AND ASPARAGUS HOLLANDAISE

3 T. cream cheese
4 T. mayonnaise
1 pkg. frozen asparagus spears
8 slices boiled ham
Toasted slivered almonds

Place cream cheese in a dish and microwave 10 seconds. Blend in mayonnaise. Microwave asparagus 3 minutes in box. Open and re-arrange spears. Microwave 3 more minutes. Spread each ham slice with cream cheese mixture and place an asparagus spear on top. Roll up ham slice and spear with toothpicks. Place on a platter; microwave 1 minute. Top with Hollandaise Sauce. Microwave 2 additional minutes and serve hot. Serves 3 to 4.

HOLLANDAISE SAUCE

¼ c. butter
¼ c. light cream
2 egg yolks, beaten
1 T. lemon juice
¼ t. salt
½ t. dry mustard

Place butter in a 2-cup measure; microwave 45 seconds to melt. Add remaining ingredients, mixing well. Microwave 1 minute, stirring every 15 seconds. Remove and beat until light.

Pictured opposite
Prize-Winning Elegant Chicken
(page 37)

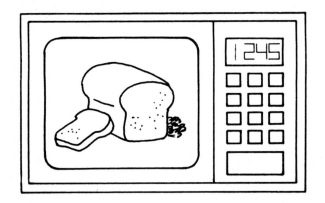

Bread

Aside from the lack of crust, breads cooked on the microwave are entirely satisfactory. They rise as high and are as moist, or more so, as breads cooked in a conventional oven. And they cook rapidly: a 9 x 5-inch loaf takes only 6½ to 7½ minutes. Bread should be turned one-half turn after half the cooking time has elapsed and removed from the pan at once to stand upside down for 3 minutes. If necessary, at this time the bread can be returned to the oven for an extra minute, right on the cooling plate.

Muffins are baked in paper-lined custard cups. Sprinkle with cinnamon-sugar for an appealing look.

Reheat bread and rolls only until the surface is warm as prolonged microwaving will dry them. Before reheating, bread should be covered with a paper towel and sweet rolls covered with plastic wrap.

GARLIC BREAD

1 loaf French bread
⅓ c. butter
½ t. garlic salt

Cut bread into ½-inch slices, not cutting through the bottom crust. Microwave butter 30 seconds to melt. Stir in garlic salt. Brush both sides of each bread slice with garlic-butter. Wrap bread in paper toweling. Microwave 45 to 60 seconds. Serves 4 to 6.

CARAMEL ROLLS

1 T. butter
1 pkg. refrigerated caramel pecan rolls

Melt butter in a 9-inch pie plate. Crumble topping from one tube of refrigerated caramel pecan rolls into the butter. Spread over the bottom of the pan. Place rolls in the dish. Microwave 3 to 3½ minutes. Let stand 1 minute. Invert dish onto plate; remove dish. Serve warm. Serves 4 to 6.

CINNAMON PUFFS

4 T. butter
1 c. biscuit mix
2 T. sugar
⅛ t. nutmeg
1 egg
¼ c. milk
¼ c. dark brown sugar
½ t. cinnamon

Place 1 tablespoon butter in a bowl. Microwave 30 seconds. Stir in biscuit mix, sugar, nutmeg, egg and milk. Beat 30 seconds. Place paper liners in cupcake holder or custard cups. Fill each liner half full. Microwave on high, uncovered, 2 to 3 minutes, turning one-quarter turn every 30 seconds. Let cool 2 to 3 minutes. Place remaining 3 tablespoons butter in a small bowl and microwave 30 seconds. Mix in sugar and cinnamon. Dip warm puffs into butter and then into sugar mixture. Serve warm. Makes 6 to 7 puffs.

To soften raisins, pour a small amount of water over raisins in a dish. Microwave, uncovered, three minutes. Let stand 2 minutes.

ENGLISH MUFFIN BREAD

5 c. flour	2½ c. milk
2 pkgs. yeast	¼ t. baking soda
1 T. sugar	1 T. warm water
2 t. salt	

In a large bowl, combine 3 cups flour, yeast, sugar and salt. In a 4-cup measure, heat milk 2 minutes. Add milk to flour, beating with mixer until smooth. Stir in remaining flour. Cover and place in a warm spot for 1 hour or until doubled in bulk. Dissolve soda in warm water. Stir down yeast batter and blend in soda mixture. Mix well. Divide batter into two 8 x 4-inch loaf dishes. Cover and let rise 45 minutes or until again doubled in bulk. Microwave each loaf 6 to 6½ minutes, uncovered, turning dish one-quarter turn every 2 minutes. Cool 5 minutes; remove from pan. Cool thoroughly. Makes 2 loaves.

BANANA MUFFINS

2 c. biscuit mix
⅓ c. sugar
1 t. cinnamon
⅛ t. nutmeg
¾ c. mashed banana
¼ c. buttermilk
1 egg, beaten
1 T. vegetable oil
12 to 26 paper cupcake liners

Combine dry ingredients in a bowl. Combine banana, buttermilk, egg and oil in another bowl. Mix with dry ingredients, stirring smooth. Fill each liner half-full. Place in microwave cupcake holder or in custard cups. Microwave 6 at a time in a circle for 2½ minutes, turning one-quarter turn every 30 seconds. Makes 12 to 26 muffins, depending on size of liners.

BRAN MUFFINS

1 c. boiling water
3 c. all-bran cereal
½ c. butter
1½ c. sugar
2 eggs
2½ c. flour
2 t. baking soda
2 c. buttermilk
½ c. raisins *or* 1 c. crushed pineapple, drained

Pour boiling water over cereal, stirring to mix. Add butter, cover and let stand until softened. Stir in sugar and eggs, beating well. Blend in flour, soda and buttermilk; mix well. Stir in raisins. Spoon into paper-lined muffin dishes or custard cups filling only one-half full. Microwave time will depend on the number of muffins cooked at a time. For 6 muffins, microwave 2¼ minutes; for 4 muffins, 2 minutes; for 2 muffins, 1¾ minutes. Makes about 60 muffins.

NOTE: Batter will keep 6 weeks in the refrigerator. Do not restir when using. Batter can be frozen cooked or uncooked in muffin liners. If batter is refrigerated, add 30 to 60 seconds cooking time.

Eggs and Cheese

Eggs are very delicate and require very little cooking time. Watch time carefully as one large egg takes only a minute to cook in the microwave oven. (Don't forget to stir a scrambled egg halfway through the cooking period; otherwise, it will be an omelet.) Egg yolks have a membrane which must be pierced before the egg is cooked or the yolk will explode. Remove eggs from the oven before they are completely done—standing time will finish the cooking. When cooking eggs, always cover the pan to retain moisture and never microwave eggs in the shell.

Cheese cooks best on medium cycle because prolonged cooking toughens it. If a dish must be cooked on high, add the cheese after most of the cooking time is up. Grated cheese melts more evenly and quickly than cheese in chunks.

WAKE-UP SPECIAL

1 T. butter
¼ c. chopped green pepper
4 eggs
½ can cream of chicken soup
5 slices bacon, cooked and crumbled
   Salt
   Pepper

Place butter and green pepper in a 2-quart casserole. Heat 30 seconds. Stir eggs and soup together and blend into butter mixture. Microwave 9 minutes on medium, stirring every 4 minutes. Crumble bacon on top and season with salt and pepper. Serves 4.

EGG AND CHEESE SOUFFLÉ

6 eggs, slightly beaten
6 slices bread, without crusts and cubed
1 c. grated Cheddar cheese
1 t. salt
1 t. dry mustard
1 lb. pork sausage, fully cooked and
   cut in pieces
2 c. milk

Mix together all ingredients and refrigerate for 12 hours. Place in a 1½-quart buttered soufflé dish. Microwave on medium cycle 50 minutes. Soufflé is done when a knife inserted in center comes out clean. Serves 6 to 8.

*Pictured opposite
Eggs Benedict
(page 44)*

CHEESE SOUFFLÉ

1 T. grated Parmesan cheese
3 T. butter
2 T. flour
¼ t. dry mustard
½ t. salt
⅛ t. pepper
   Dash cayenne
1 c. milk
1 c. plus 2 T. shredded sharp Cheddar
   cheese
5 egg whites, room temperature
¼ t. cream of tartar
4 egg yolks

Butter a 1½-quart soufflé dish; sprinkle with Parmesan cheese. Place butter, flour, mustard, salt, pepper and cayenne in a large mixing bowl. Heat, uncovered, 1 minute; stir well. Gradually stir in milk. Heat, uncovered, 2 to 3 minutes until thickened, stirring every minute to keep mixture smooth. Add 1 cup Cheddar; stir until melted. Beat 5 egg whites with cream of tartar until stiff, but not dry. Set aside. Beat egg yolks until thick and lemon colored; add to cheese sauce. Beat well. Gently fold in about a quarter of the egg whites into the sauce, working quickly. Fold in remaining egg whites. Carefully pour into soufflé dish. Sprinkle with the remaining 2 tablespoons Cheddar cheese. Place soufflé dish in an 8-inch square dish to which has been added 2 inches water. Cover with waxed paper. Microwave on medium 10 to 11 minutes, turning dish one-half turn after 5 minutes. Let stand in hot water until ready to serve. Serves 6 to 8.

FRIED EGGS

Preheat browning skillet 1 minute. Add 1 teaspoon butter, then add egg. Pierce yolk with a toothpick. Cover and microwave 30 seconds for a "sunny-side-up" egg; 45 seconds for an "easy-over" egg (do not flip egg over). For an egg with a solid yolk, microwave egg 1 minute.

EGGS BENEDICT

1 pkg. frozen asparagus spears
2 English muffins, split and toasted
4 slices ham
4 poached eggs
   Hollandaise Sauce

Microwave asparagus in package for 3 minutes. Open and rearrange asparagus spears. Close package and microwave an additional 2 to 3 minutes. Drain. Place 1 muffin half on each of 4 plates with 1 slice ham on each muffin. Arrange asparagus on top of ham, dividing equally between servings. Microwave 2 at a time, uncovered, 45 to 60 seconds. Top with poached egg and Hollandaise Sauce (p. 39).

SWISS CHEESE DELIGHT

2 eggs, slightly beaten
1 c. milk
¼ t. salt
¼ t. paprika
   Dash cayenne
½ t. dry mustard
4 slices white bread
½ lb. Swiss cheese, grated

Beat eggs; add milk and seasonings. Pour egg mixture into a square baking dish. Dip slices of bread into mixture, coating both sides. Grate cheese and sprinkle over bread slices. Microwave on low 14 minutes. Serves 4.

When a recipe directs you to cover dishes in the microwave oven, use either plastic wrap or glass casserole lids.

OMELET WITH MELBA SAUCE

3 eggs, separated	Dash pepper
3 T. sour cream	2 t. butter
½ t. salt	

Beat egg whites until stiff, but not dry. Beat egg yolks slightly and stir in sour cream, salt and pepper. Fold egg yolk mixture into egg whites. Melt 1 teaspoon butter in each of 2 bowls, spreading over the bottom of each dish. Pour half of egg mixture in each bowl. Place both bowls in oven and microwave 1 minute on high, then 7 minutes on medium. Slide omelets onto plates and top with hot Melba Sauce. Serves 4.

MELBA SAUCE

1 10-oz. pkg. whole frozen raspberries, thawed
2 t. cornstarch
1 t. Grand Marnier
Sour cream for garnish

Drain raspberry juice into a small bowl. Set berries aside. Add cornstarch to the juice, stirring to dissolve. Microwave 3 minutes, stirring twice. Stir in Grand Marnier and whole berries. Cover; microwave 1½ minutes, stirring after 45 seconds. Let stand, covered, for 1 minute. Serve with a dollop of sour cream.

TOMATO CHEESE RAREBIT

1 10½-oz. can tomato soup
1 lb. American cheese, grated
2 eggs, separated
¼ t. paprika
1 t. brown sugar
Dash cayenne
Hot toasted French bread

In a 2-quart casserole, combine tomato soup and grated cheese. Cover and microwave 10 minutes on medium cycle, stirring after 5 minutes. Beat egg yolks with paprika, brown sugar and cayenne. Stir into soup mixture. Microwave 1 minute. Beat egg whites until stiff but not dry. Fold into cooked mixture and pour over hot toasted French bread. Serves 4.

SCRAMBLED EGG

Melt 1 teaspoon butter in a dish. Stir in egg and 1 teaspoon water or milk, if desired. Microwave 30 seconds; stir. Microwave 15 seconds.

> If a range of cooking time is given in a recipe, always cook for the shortest time. Then give the food its standing time. If an extra minute or two is needed, it can be added now.

EGG FOO YUNG SCRAMBLE

6 eggs
1 can bean sprouts, drained
½ c. chopped onion
¼ c. chopped green pepper
2 T. soy sauce
2 T. butter

Beat eggs in a 2-quart casserole. Add remaining ingredients. Cover and microwave 5½ minutes. Stir after 2½ minutes and again after 4 minutes. Let stand, covered, for 2 minutes. Serves 6 to 8.

POACHED EGG

In a 10-ounce custard cup, microwave ¼ cup water and ¼ teaspoon vinegar to a boil, about one minute. Slip egg into the water. Cover with plastic wrap and microwave 10 to 15 seconds. Let stand 30 to 60 seconds.

Sandwiches

To heat a sandwich, first wrap it in a paper napkin to absorb extra moisture and heat for 20 to 30 seconds. Sandwiches should be cut in half and the centers turned to the outside where they will get the most microwave power. Heat sandwiches or food from fast-food restaurants in the containers in which they come if the containers do not contain metal or have metal handles.

DEVILED DOG SANDWICHES /HIGH\

6 slices bacon
6 hot dogs
1 2¼-oz. can deviled ham
½ c. shredded sharp Cheddar cheese
2 T. chopped, pitted ripe olives
1 t. dry mustard
6 frankfurter rolls

Place bacon between layers of paper towels and microwave 3½ to 4 minutes (bacon will not be crisp). Split hot dogs lengthwise, not cutting all the way through. Mix together ham, cheese, olives and mustard. Spread on inside of hot dogs and press together. Wrap 1 slice of bacon around each hot dog and place in roll. Wrap sandwich loosely in a paper towel. Place 3 sandwiches 1 inch apart in the oven. Microwave 1½ to 2 minutes. Repeat other 3 sandwiches. Serves 3 to 4.

DENVER SANDWICH /HIGH\

1 egg
1 T. chopped green pepper
2 T. chopped onion
3 T. chopped ham
  Toasted English muffin

Combine all ingredients except muffin; mix well. Pour onto a small plate. Microwave 1 minute and place on bun. Serves 1.

REUBEN /HIGH\

Rye bread
Sauerkraut
Sliced corned beef
Swiss cheese
Thousand Island dressing
Butter

Spread 1 side of each slice bread with butter. Place corned beef on unbuttered side, add sauerkraut, Swiss cheese and dressing. Place second piece of bread on top, buttered side out. Preheat browning skillet 2½ minutes. Place sandwich in skillet. Microwave 45 seconds; turn sandwich over and microwave 45 seconds. Make as many as desired.

SOUPY BURGERS /HIGH\

1 lb. ground round
½ c. chopped onion
1 10½-oz. can chicken gumbo soup
2 T. catsup
1 t. mustard
½ t. salt
¼ t. pepper
6 hamburger rolls
6 slices American cheese

Combine meat and onion in a 1½-quart casserole. Cover and microwave 2½ minutes. Stir and microwave, covered, another 2½ minutes. Add remaining ingredients except rolls. Microwave 1½ minutes. Spoon onto rolls and top with a slice of cheese. Place on a paper towel-lined plate, top with another paper towel. Microwave 20 to 30 seconds. Serves 6.

Pictured opposite
Deviled Dog Sandwiches

Desserts

You will find your microwave is an invaluable tool in making desserts. You can use it for a variety of tasks, including melting butter and making gelatin. Chocolate melts quickly and without scorching. Many people believe fruit desserts—crisps and cobblers—are tastier in the microwave since the fruit cooks quickly and retains all its flavor.

COFFEE-MALLOW TORTONI

1 c. miniature marshmallows
½ c. milk
1 t. instant coffee crystals
¼ c. chopped toasted almonds
2 egg whites
½ t. vanilla
2 T. sugar
½ c. heavy cream, whipped

In a 4-cup measure, combine marshmallows and milk. Microwave, uncovered, 1½ to 2 minutes. Stir to blend. Stir in coffee crystals. Chill until partially set. Stir in nuts. Beat egg whites and vanilla until soft peaks form. Gradually add sugar. Beat to stiff peaks. Fold egg whites and cream into coffee mixture. Spoon into paper-lined muffin cups. Freeze. Serves 6 to 8.

APPLE CRISP

5 c. peeled apple slices
¼ c. orange juice
½ c. raisins
⅓ c. butter
¾ c. brown sugar
½ c. flour
½ c. regular or quick-cooking oats
¼ c. chopped nuts

Combine apple slices and orange juice in an 8-inch round dish. Stir in raisins and set aside. Place butter in a mixing bowl and microwave 30 to 45 seconds. Blend butter, brown sugar, flour, oats and nuts until crumbly. Sprinkle over apples. Cover and microwave 12 to 15 minutes. Turn dish one-quarter turn every 2 minutes. Let stand, covered, 5 minutes. Serves 6 to 8.

LIME SOUFFLÉ

1 T. unflavored gelatin
½ c. sugar
½ t. salt
1 c. water
4 eggs, separated
1 T. grated lime peel
⅓ c. lime juice
5 drops green food coloring
¼ c. sugar
1 c. heavy cream
¼ c. sugar

Prepare a 4-cup soufflé dish by forming a 3-inch collar of waxed paper around the top edge of the dish. Press waxed paper strip against lightly greased inside of dish. Allow to extend 2 inches above the dish. Combine gelatin, ½ cup sugar and salt in a 4-cup measure. Add water. Beat yolks slightly and blend in. Microwave 4 to 5 minutes until mixture bubbles, stirring every 2 minutes. Beat smooth. Stir in lime peel and juice. Cool until thickened but not set. Add food coloring. Beat egg whites until frothy. Gradually add ¼ cup sugar and beat to soft peaks; set aside. Whip cream until thick; stir in ¼ cup sugar. Fold cream and gelatin into egg whites. Spoon into soufflé dish. Refrigerate 4 hours. Remove collar and serve. Serves 6 to 8.

SOME-MORES

Break graham cracker in half. Top half of the cracker with a piece of chocolate bar. Place a marshmallow on top of the chocolate. Microwave 6 at a time 30 to 40 seconds. Top with other half of each cracker. Serve.

JELLO

1 3-oz. pkg. gelatin
1 c. water
1 c. fruit juice

Place gelatin powder and water in a 2-cup measure. Stir well. Microwave to boiling, 3 to 4 minutes. Remove from oven and stir well. Add fruit juice. Refrigerate until thickened. Serves 4.

PUDDING MIX

In a 4-cup measuring cup place 2 cups milk and 3¼-oz. package of any flavor pudding mix. Mix. Microwave 3 minutes and stir well. Microwave 2 to 4 more minutes, stirring well at the end of each minute. Cool and serve. Serves 4.

RHUBARB CRISP

4 c. rhubarb	1 c. brown sugar
½ c. sugar	1 c. flour
2 T. lemon juice	½ c. butter
½ t. lemon rind	

Mix rhubarb, sugar, lemon juice and rind. Place in an 8-inch square dish. Mix brown sugar, flour and butter until crumbly. Sprinkle over rhubarb. Cover and microwave 12 to 15 minutes, turning dish one-quarter turn every 2 minutes. Serves 4 to 6.

APPLE STRUDEL

4 phylo leaves
¼ c. butter
½ c. fine bread crumbs
3 apples, chopped
½ c. sugar
¼ c. raisins
½ c. dried apricots
¼ c. chopped nuts
   Grated rind of 1 lemon
   Juice of ½ lemon
   Cinnamon-sugar mixture

Unfold 2 phylo leaves and place on a damp cloth. Microwave butter 30 seconds to melt. Brush leaves with butter. Place second leaf on top of the first leaf. Sprinkle bread crumbs on the second leaf. Repeat with other two leaves to make a second strudel. Combine apples, sugar, raisins, apricots, nuts, lemon rind and juice, mixing well. Place half of this mixture in the center of each strudel. Roll up as for a jelly roll. Brush pastry with butter and sprinkle with cinnamon-sugar mixture. Microwave each strudel 8 to 9 minutes, basting with butter. Cool. Cut each into 16 pieces. Serves 8 to 10.

ORANGE FROZEN YOGURT

1 3-oz. pkg. orange gelatin
¾ c. sugar
1 c. water
1 c. fresh orange juice
2 8-oz. cartons plain yogurt
1 c. heavy cream, whipped

Combine gelatin, sugar and water in a 4-cup measure. Stir well. Microwave 1½ to 2 minutes until boiling. Stir once. Cool 30 minutes. Stir in yogurt and orange juice. Place in a 13 x 9-inch dish. Freeze, stirring occasionally so it freezes evenly. Freeze 2 to 3 hours. Beat this on medium with a mixer until smooth. Fold in whipped cream. Pour in freezer container. Cover and freeze until firm, 3 to 4 hours. Serves 6.

CHOCOLATE ANGEL DELIGHT

¼ c. cold water
1 envelope unflavored gelatin
¼ c. water
1 12-oz. pkg. semisweet chocolate chips
6 eggs, separated
¼ c. sugar
1 t. vanilla
4 c. heavy cream, whipped
1 c. chopped nuts
2 qts. bite-size pieces angel food cake
Shaved chocolate for garnish
Cherries for garnish

Place ¼ cup cold water in a measuring cup. Sprinkle gelatin on top and mix. Microwave 15 to 30 seconds; stir. Cool. In a 4-cup measure, place chocolate chips and the ¼ cup water. Microwave 2 minutes; stir until smooth. Cool chocolate mixture. Beat whites until stiff, but not dry. Beat yolks with ¼ cup sugar. Fold in chocolate mixture, egg whites, vanilla, whipped cream, nuts and gelatin. Spoon 2 cups chocolate mixture into a 10-inch tube pan. Sprinkle with cake. Alternate layers of chocolate mixture and cake, pressing cake into the chocolate. Chill firm. Garnish with shaved chocolate and cherries. Serves 12 to 16.

FROZEN BERRY YOGURT

1 envelope unflavored gelatin
¼ c. orange juice
½ c. grenadine
1 pt. fresh strawberries, washed and hulled
2 8-oz. cartons plain yogurt
½ c. sour cream
2 egg whites
¼ c. sugar

Sprinkle gelatin over orange juice in small cup. Wait 5 minutes. Microwave 20 seconds. Stir well. Cool. Combine grenadine, strawberries, yogurt and sour cream. Place in blender. Blend until smooth. Blend in gelatin. Pour into a 9 x 9 x 2-inch pan. Freeze (about 2 to 3 hours), stirring a few times so it freezes evenly. Beat egg whites until foamy and double in volume. Beat in sugar, 1 tablespoon at a time until meringue forms stiff peaks. Beat frozen mixture with mixer until smooth. Fold in meringue. Pour into freezer container. Freeze about 2 hours. Remove 15 minutes before serving. Serves 6.

AMBROSIA CRISP

1 10-oz. pkg. frozen strawberries, thawed
1 8¼-oz. can pineapple chunks
6 T. brown sugar
1 T. cornstarch
1 11-oz. can mandarin orange slices, drained
¼ c. shredded coconut
¼ c. quick-cooking oats
2 T. flour
⅛ t. cinnamon
2 T. butter

Drain strawberries and pineapple, reserving syrup. Combine syrups to make 1 cup liquid. In a 10 x 6-inch dish, mix 2 tablespoons of the sugar with the cornstarch. Slowly blend in the juices. Microwave, uncovered, 3 to 4 minutes, stirring after each minute. Add fruits and coconut. Mix remaining sugar, oats, flour and cinnamon. Cut in remaining butter. Sprinkle over fruits. Microwave, uncovered, 3 minutes, turning dish one-half turn after 1½ minutes. Serves 6 to 8.

Pictured opposite
Chocolate Angel Delight (this page)
Brandy Alexander Pie (page 53)

Pie

Since microwaves cook the edges of food first, proceeding toward the center, it becomes necessary to stir custard-type pie fillings for even cooking. Every two minutes for the first three-quarters of the cooking time, use a spoon to gently pull the cooked edges toward the center, allowing the uncooked portions to flow to the edges. Allow to remain undisturbed for the last quarter of the cooking time.

Pie crusts are very delicate and must be turned every 30 seconds during the cooking cycle. Always cook shells for 2½ minutes before filling so they will not be soggy.

There are two methods for cooking pie shells: The first is to place the shell in a 9-inch pie pan, cover with a paper towel, and place an eight-inch pie dish on the paper towel. Cook 2½ minutes, turning every thirty seconds. Remove from oven and immediately remove the eight-inch pie dish and the paper towel.

The other method is to place shell in a pie dish and prick it thoroughly with a fork. Cook for 2½ minutes, turning every 30 seconds.

The benefit of using the first method is that you do not have to prick the crust. This is important when you think a thin pie filling will leak out through the prick holes.

Frozen pie shells may be cooked using either of the above methods. Remember to remove them from their foil pan and place them in a pie dish suitable for use in the microwave oven.

For added color, make your pie crust with a yellow colored margarine and milk. Then, before cooking the pie, brush the crust with slightly beaten egg white to which a few drops of water have been added. You may also sprinkle the crust with cinnamon-sugar.

BRANDY ALEXANDER PIE

¼ c. butter
1½ c. vanilla wafer crumbs
3 c. miniature marshmallows
½ c. milk
¼ c. creme de cacao
¼ c. cognac
1 c. heavy cream, whipped
Semisweet chocolate to garnish

Place butter in a 9-inch pie plate; microwave 30 to 45 seconds to melt. Stir in wafer crumbs. Press into bottom and up sides of pie plate. Microwave 2 minutes, turning dish every 30 seconds. Cool. In a large bowl, mix marshmallows and milk. Microwave 3 to 4 minutes; stirring smooth. Beat in creme de cacao and cognac. Chill 30 minutes, stirring once or twice. Fold in whipped cream and pour onto crust. Cover; chill 4 hours. Peel chocolate with vegetable peeler and let curls fall onto pie. Makes one 9-inch pie.

APPLE CRUMBLE PIE

5 large apples, peeled and sliced
¼ c. brown sugar
1 t. cinnamon
1 9-inch pie shell
½ c. brown sugar
¾ c. flour
⅓ c. butter

Combine apples, ¼ cup brown sugar and cinnamon. Pour into pie shell. Mix together remaining brown sugar and flour; cut in butter. Spoon over top of apples. Microwave 6 to 8 minutes, turning pie one-quarter turn every 2 minutes. Serves 8.

PIE CRUST

1 t. salt   ¾ c. shortening
2¼ c. sifted flour   5 T. cold water

Mix salt and flour. Cut in shortening with a pastry blender. Sprinkle over cold water, mixing with a fork until dough holds together. Divide into 2 balls. Roll out each on a well-floured board. Place in a 9-inch pie plate. Prick crust with tines of fork. Microwave on medium 7 to 9 minutes, turning dish one-quarter turn every 3 minutes. Makes two 9-inch crusts.

GRASSHOPPER TARTS

1 4-oz. bar milk chocolate
2 T. butter
20 large marshmallows
⅓ c. milk
2 T. white creme de cacao
2 T. green creme de menthe
½ c. heavy cream, whipped

Make a few chocolate curls for garnish by peeling thin layers of chocolate with a vegetable peeler. Set aside. Microwave remaining chocolate and butter in a 2-cup glass casserole for 1 to 1½ minutes until soft. Stir smooth. Divide chocolate between 6 paper-lined custard cups. Using the back of a spoon, spread chocolate evenly over the bottom and up the sides of paper lining. Refrigerate or freeze until set. Combine marshmallows and milk in a glass casserole. Microwave 1¼ to 1½ minutes until puffed. Stir smooth. Blend in creme de menthe and creme de cacao. Refrigerate 45 minutes. Fold in whipped cream. Spoon into chocolate cups. Chill 2 to 3 hours. Remove tarts from paper liners and peel off paper. Top with additional whipped cream and chocolate curls.

CHOCOLATE ALMOND PIE

1 3¾-oz. milk chocolate bar with almonds
15 large marshmallows
½ c. milk
1 c. heavy cream, whipped
1 9-inch graham cracker crust

Break chocolate bar into pieces. Combine with milk and marshmallows in a 1-quart casserole. Microwave 2 to 3 minutes, stirring every 30 seconds. Stir until smooth. Cool. Fold in whipped cream and pour into crust. Chill 3 hours. Makes one 9-inch pie.

VANILLA CRUMB CRUST

1½ c. vanilla wafer crumbs
¼ c. melted butter

Place butter in a 9-inch pie plate. Microwave 30 seconds to melt. Stir in cookie crumbs. Press buttered crumbs into bottom and sides of pie plate. Microwave 2 minutes. Makes one 9-inch pie crust.

LEMONADE PIE

1 9-inch Graham-Nut Crust, cooled
¾ c. cold water
1 T. unflavored gelatin
⅔ c. sugar
¼ t. salt
1 6-oz. can frozen lemonade concentrate
1 3-oz. pkg. cream cheese
1 pt. heavy cream, whipped
   Yellow food coloring

Combine water and gelatin in a 4-cup measure. Let stand to soften. Add sugar and salt. Microwave 1¼ to 2 minutes. Stir in lemonade concentrate; set aside. Microwave cream cheese in a bowl 15 to 30 seconds; beat creamy. Add lemonade mixture, mixing smooth. Refrigerate to thicken. Fold in whipped cream and coloring. Pour onto crust. Refrigerate overnight. Makes one 9-inch pie.

GRAHAM-NUT CRUST

¼ c. butter
1¼ c. graham cracker crumbs
2 T. sugar
2 T. chopped nuts

Microwave butter 45 seconds to melt. Add crumbs, sugar and nuts. Press into a 9-inch pie plate. Microwave 2 to 2½ minutes, turning dish every 30 seconds.

BANANA PIE

1 9-inch vanilla crumb crust, baked
1 3-oz. pkg. vanilla pudding
1¾ c. milk
1½ c. miniature marshmallows
1 9-oz. container whipped topping
2 bananas, sliced
   Cherries for garnish

Mix pudding and milk in a 1-quart casserole; stir. Microwave 2 minutes. Stir and microwave an additional 3 to 3½ minutes, stirring every minute. Cover with waxed paper and chill thoroughly. Whip pudding and fold in topping and marshmallows. Arrange half the banana slices in pie shell. Pour in filling. Garnish pie with remaining banana slices and cherries. Makes one 9-inch pie.

SPECKLED HOLIDAY PIE

¼ c. butter
¼ c. corn syrup
½ c. semisweet chocolate chips
2 c. Special K cereal
1½ 8-oz. pkgs. cream cheese, softened
¾ c. sugar
2 T. brandy
½ c. quartered maraschino cherries
½ c. chopped almonds
4½ c. heavy cream, whipped
   Cherry halves for garnish

Combine butter, corn syrup and chocolate chips in a casserole. Microwave 1 to 2 minutes; stir smooth. Add cereal, stirring to coat. Press into a greased 9-inch pie plate. Chill. Beat cream cheese and sugar until smooth. Add brandy; fold in remaining ingredients. Spread onto crust. Garnish with cherry halves. Freeze 4 hours. Let stand at room temperature 15 minutes before cutting. Makes one 9-inch pie.

NOTE: To soften cream cheese, place on a plate and microwave 45 to 60 seconds.

PUMPKIN PIE

2 eggs
½ c. sugar
½ c. firmly packed dark brown sugar
1 T. flour
½ t. salt
1 t. cinnamon
¼ t. nutmeg
¼ t. ginger
¼ t. allspice
1 16-oz. can pumpkin
1 14-oz. can evaporated milk
1 baked 12-inch pie shell

In large mixing bowl, combine all ingredients (except pastry shell) in order given. Beat until well blended. Pour mixture into pie shell. Microwave, uncovered, 4 minutes until edges begin to set. With a spoon, carefully pull the cooked portions to the center of the dish. Microwave, uncovered, an additional 6 to 8 minutes. Let stand 5 minutes. Turn pie plate one-half turn after 3 minutes and again pull cooked portions to center. Pie is done when knife inserted in center comes out clean. Cool. Makes one 9-inch pie.

Pictured opposite
Citrus Nut Cake (page 57)

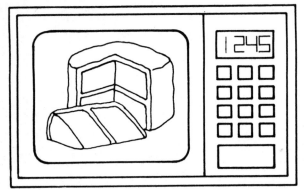

Cake

Cakes are extra easy in a microwave; an 8-inch layer cooks in only 6½ minutes and an 8 x 12-inch loaf cooks in 12 to 14 minutes. A bundt cake is done in 13½ to 14 minutes.

Cakes must be turned a quarter turn every 2½ minutes to eliminate the "hills and valleys" on the top. Bundt pans are ideal for the microwave since there is no center which microwaves would reach last. Round pans are preferred for cakes. If you must use a square pan, the cake should be shielded 6 minutes into the cooking time. To do this, wrap 3 thicknesses of aluminum foil around the outside of the pan, the foil being the same height of the pan. This shield deflects the microwaves toward the center of the cake.

Because there is no long, hot cooking to cause cakes to stick to the pans, they slip out easily even if you do not grease and flour the pans. For extra ease in removing, place a flattened paper coffee filter on the bottom of each pan before pouring in batter. After turning cake out, immediately remove filter.

To test cake, stick a toothpick into the cake at a point half way between the center and the edge. If it comes out clean, the cake is done. If the cake appears moist when it comes from the oven, place a piece of waxed paper over the moist spots; the cake will continue cooking under the paper.

HOLIDAY GREEN CAKE

1 c. chopped pecans
¾ c. sugar
2 T. cinnamon
1 white cake mix
1 3-oz. pkg. instant pistachio pudding
4 large eggs
1 c. sour cream
¾ c. orange juice
¼ c. vegetable oil
1 t. vanilla

Mix together pecans, sugar and cinnamon. Sprinkle one-third of the pecan mixture into the bottom and up the sides of 10-inch bundt cake pan. In an electric mixer, blend together remaining ingredients and beat 5 minutes. Alternately layer batter and remaining nut mixture; swirl with a fork. Microwave 13 to 15 minutes, turning dish one-quarter turn every 2 minutes. Cool 15 to 20 minutes in the pan; turn out. Makes one 10-inch bundt cake.

HOLIDAY FRUITCAKE /Med

¾ c. unsifted flour
¾ t. baking powder
¾ t. nutmeg
¾ t. salt
¾ t. allspice
1¾ c. diced green candied cherries
1¾ c. diced red candied cherries
6 c. coarsely chopped walnuts
¾ c. butter, room temperature
6 T. dark brown sugar
3 T. honey
6 eggs
6 T. brandy

Sift together flour, baking powder, nutmeg, salt and allspice. Set aside. Combine cherries and walnuts. Set aside. Cream butter; add sugar and honey. Beat in eggs, one at a time. Add flour mixture and beat smooth. Add brandy, mixing well. Fold in nut mixture. Pour into a 1½-quart soufflé dish. Cover with waxed paper. Microwave on medium 16 to 18 minutes, turning dish one-quarter turn every 2 minutes. Let stand 20 minutes. Makes one 8-inch cake.

CITRUS-NUT CAKE

1 c. butter
1 c. sugar
3 egg yolks
2 c. sifted flour
1 t. baking powder
1 t. baking soda
½ pt. sour cream
½ c. chopped pecans
    Grated rind of 1 fresh orange
2 T. fresh orange juice
3 egg whites, beaten stiff

Cream butter and sugar; add egg yolks. Mix together flour, baking powder, soda; add alternately with sour cream. Stir in pecans, orange rind and orange juice. Fold in egg whites. Place a coffee filter paper in the bottom of an 8-inch round glass dish. Fill half full with batter. Microwave 6½ minutes, turning one-fourth turn every 2 minutes. Remove from oven; turn out onto plate. Remove liner. Brush with Glaze, top with Topping and decorate with whole pecans and orange slices. Makes one 8-inch cake.

NOTE: Use remaining batter to make cupcakes, filling cups half full. Place liners in microwave cupcake plastic dish or in custard dishes. Microwave 6 cupcakes at a time, 2½ minutes, turning one-fourth turn every 30 seconds. When cool, glaze and top as for cake.

GLAZE

½ c. sugar
½ c. orange juice
1 T. Cointreau

Combine all ingredients, mixing well.

TOPPING

1 9-oz. container whipped topping
1 T. Cointreau

Stir flavoring into whipped topping. Spread on cake and garnish with whole pecans and orange slices.

> To soften refrigerated icing to spreading consistency, microwave, uncovered, 15 to 20 seconds per cup. Fifteen seconds will liquefy honey or syrup for serving.

BLACK RUSSIAN CAKE

1 chocolate cake mix
1 3-oz. pkg. instant pudding mix
4 eggs
¼ c. Kahlua
¼ c. vodka
¾ c. light cream

Mix together all ingredients and beat 6 minutes. Pour into a bundt pan or two 9-inch round pans lined with flattened paper coffee filter. Microwave 11 to 14 minutes in bundt pan or 6½ minutes for round pans. Turn one-quarter turn every 2 minutes. Cool and frost with Black Russian Icing. Makes one 10-inch bundt cake.

BLACK RUSSIAN ICING

1 1-lb. box confectioners' sugar
2 T. vodka
2 T. Kahlua
2 T. light cream
2 T. butter

In a bowl, mix all ingredients except butter. Place butter in middle of batter. Microwave 1 to 2 minutes, stirring after 30 to 45 seconds. Beat until smooth, mixing in butter.

CHEESECAKE

1 9-inch crumb crust
½ of a 16-oz. pkg. marshmallows
½ c. milk
1 8-oz. pkg. cream cheese
½ pt. heavy cream

Combine marshmallows and milk in a bowl; microwave 3 to 4 minutes to melt. Microwave cream cheese 45 seconds to soften. Beat cream cheese into milk mixture; cool. Whip cream until stiff; fold into milk mixture. Pour onto crust and refrigerate several hours. Serve topped with thawed frozen strawberries. Makes one 9-inch cake.

PEANUT ICING

1 c. brown sugar
½ c. chunky peanut butter
2 T. softened butter
2 T. milk
1 c. peanuts

Place all ingredients except peanuts in a 1-quart casserole. Microwave 1 to 2 minutes; stir. Microwave 1 more minute, until mixture boils. Add peanuts and spread on cake. Enough to frost a 1-layer cake.

Cookies and Bars

A twelve-inch, corrugated cardboard cake circle makes an excellent cookie sheet. Cover with a piece of waxed paper and place cookies around outer edge. Do not place any cookies in the center. Turn the circle once during cooking. Microwave 12 cookies 2½ minutes on high or 4½ to 5½ minutes on medium cycle.

CARAMEL APPLE SQUARES

CRUST

½ c. butter	¼ c. sugar
1½ c. flour	1 egg yolk

FILLING

30 caramels
2 T. water
6 medium apples, peeled and sliced
1 T. lemon juice

TOPPING

1 c. flour	½ c. butter
⅓ c. brown sugar	Cinnamon-sugar

Microwave ½ cup butter for 45 seconds to melt. Blend into flour, sugar and egg yolk. Press into the bottom of 12 x 8 x 2-inch dish. Microwave 5 to 6 minutes. Turn dish one-half turn after 2½ minutes. Unwrap caramels and place in a dish with water. Microwave 2 to 2½ minutes, stirring twice during cooking process. Arrange apples on crust. Drizzle with lemon juice and caramel mixture. Make Topping by combining flour and brown sugar; cut in butter. Sprinkle over apples. Sprinkle top with cinnamon-sugar. Microwave 10 to 12 minutes; cool. Makes 24 bars.

PUMPKIN BARS

¼ c. butter	½ t. baking powder
¾ c. brown sugar	½ t. salt
2 eggs	¼ t. baking soda
1 t. vanilla	½ t. cinnamon
1 c. pumpkin	½ t. nutmeg
1 c. flour	¼ t. ginger

Microwave butter for 30 seconds to melt. Blend in brown sugar. Add eggs, one at a time, beating after each addition. Blend in remaining ingredients; mix smooth. Lightly grease bottom only of a 12 x 8 x 2-inch pan. Spread mixture evenly. Microwave 8 to 9½ minutes, shielding bars after 4 minutes and turning dish every 2 minutes. Cool. Spread Icing on bars and sprinkle on nuts. Makes 24 bars.

ICING

1 3-oz. pkg. cream cheese
1 T. butter
2 c. confectioners' sugar
1 T. milk
Chopped nuts

Microwave cream cheese and butter for 20 to 30 seconds. Add sugar and milk, blending smooth.

GRAHAM-CHOCOLATE TREATS

1½ c. graham cracker crumbs
1 can sweetened condensed milk
1 c. semisweet chocolate chips
1 c. chopped nuts

Combine all ingredients. Spread in an ungreased 8-inch square glass dish. Microwave 6½ to 7½ minutes. Turn dish 45 degrees every 2 minutes. Cool 1 hour; cut into 24 bars.

OATMEAL BARS

4 c. rolled oats
1 c. brown sugar
1 c. softened butter
⅔ c. white corn syrup

Combine oats and brown sugar; cut in butter. Stir in syrup and press into two 8-inch round baking dishes. Microwave each 3½ minutes, turning dish one-quarter turn after 2 minutes. Remove from oven and spread with Topping. Cool and cut into squares. Makes 32 bars.

TOPPING

1 c. peanut butter
1 12-oz. pkg. chocolate chips

Microwave peanut butter and chocolate chips 2 minutes to melt. Stir at half time.

CANDY-TOPPED BROWNIES

½ c. butter	1 c. flour
½ c. brown sugar	¼ t. salt

Microwave ½ cup butter 30 seconds to melt. Blend in ½ cup brown sugar, flour and salt until crumbly. Press into an 8-inch square dish. Microwave 3 to 3½ minutes, turning dish twice. Top with Topping. Makes 16 squares.

TOPPING

¾ c. brown sugar
¼ c. butter
2 T. milk
¾ t. vanilla
½ c. chopped nuts

Combine ¾ cup brown sugar, ¼ cup butter and milk. Microwave 3 minutes, stirring twice. Add vanilla. Pour over crust and sprinkle with nuts. Microwave 2 to 2½ minutes.

GRANOLA BARS

½ c. honey
¾ c. peanut butter
3 c. granola
½ c. chopped nuts
⅓ c. dried apricots or raisins
¼ c. toasted sunflower seeds
¼ c. coconut
¼ c. wheat germ
¼ c. toasted sesame seed

In a 3-quart bowl, bring honey to a boil and boil for 1 minute. Add peanut butter and blend; microwave 30 seconds. In a separate bowl, mix remaining ingredients. Stir into hot honey mixture. Press into a 7 x 11 x 2-inch dish. Cover and chill. Makes 24 bars.

NOTE: To toast sesame seeds, spread in a 7 x 11 x 2-inch dish. Microwave 5 minutes until golden, stirring 3 times.

LEMON BARS

½ c. melted margarine
1 pkg. lemon cake mix
3 eggs
1 8-oz. pkg. softened cream cheese
1 box lemon frosting mix

Microwave butter 45 seconds to melt. Add cake mix and one slightly beaten egg. Mix with a fork. Press into two 8-inch round glass dishes. Blend frosting mix into cream cheese. Set aside ½ cup. Add 2 eggs to remaining frosting mix; beat 5 minutes. Spread over 2 cakes. Microwave each 6½ minutes, turning one-quarter turn every 2 minutes. Cool. Spread with reserved frosting mixture. Makes 24 bars.

MARSHMALLOW CEREAL TREATS

¼ c. butter
5 c. crisp rice cereal
4 c. miniature marshmallows

Place butter and marshmallows in a 3-quart bowl. Microwave 3 minutes, stirring often until creamy. Add cereal and mix thoroughly. Press into a buttered 9 x 12 x 2-inch dish. Cool. Cut into 40 squares.

Candy

When making candy in a microwave, there is no more constant stirring or watching a thermometer. Now, all you have to do is listen for the timer. Be sure to use a bowl large enough and deep enough as the sugar syrup can boil over the sides of a too-shallow dish.

To melt chocolate, place 8 ounces of broken chocolate in a 4-cup glass measure. Heat 2 minutes; remove from oven. The chocolate will look just as it did when it went into the oven; but stirring thins it. If more time is needed to melt, stir first then add additional time in 30-second intervals.

Caramels are easily melted. Add 2 tablespoons water per 14 ounces of caramels. Microwave 2 minutes; stir until smooth. Use for dipping apples or roll in chopped nuts. If caramel stiffens before you have used it, microwave an additional 10 to 15 seconds.

CARAMEL FUDGE

1½ c. sugar
⅓ c. milk
¼ c. butter or margarine
1 14-oz. bag caramels
¾ c. chopped nuts

In a large glass bowl, combine sugar, milk and butter. Microwave 2 minutes. Mix well and microwave 5 minutes, stirring twice during cooking. Add caramels; microwave 45 to 60 seconds. Beat until caramels are melted and mixture is smooth. Stir in nuts. Pour into a lightly greased 8-inch square dish. Cool. Cut into pieces. Enough for 16 pieces.

CHOCOLATE EASTER NESTS /HIGH

1 9¾-oz. bar milk chocolate
1 4-oz. bar sweet baking chocolate
½ c. shredded coconut
2 c. crushed cornflakes
Jelly beans

Put chocolate into large bowl. Microwave 2 to 3 minutes. Stir. Add coconut and cornflakes. Spoon onto waxed paper and form into nests. Decorate with 2 to 3 jelly beans in each nest. Makes 16 nests.

CHINESE CHEWS /HIGH

1 6-oz. pkg. chocolate chips
1 6-oz. pkg. butterscotch chips
1 3-oz. can chow mein noodles
1 6½-oz. jar peanuts

Place all chips in a 2-quart bowl. Microwave 2 to 3 minutes to melt. Stir smooth. Add noodles and nuts, stirring to coat well. Drop onto waxed paper by teaspoonfuls. Put in freezer to set quickly. Makes 48 bars.

PEANUT BUTTER CANDY /HIGH

1½ c. smooth peanut butter
1¾ c. brown sugar
1¾ c. confectioners' sugar
¼ to ½ c. melted butter
1 c. chocolate chips
¼ c. butter

Combine peanut butter, sugars and melted butter, mixing well. Spread into a buttered 9 x 13 x 2-inch baking dish. Place chocolate chips and butter in a 4-cup measure. Microwave 2 minutes. Remove from oven; stir until creamy. Spread over peanut butter mixture. Cool and cut into squares. Makes 24 squares.

NOTE: When using a thick peanut butter, it may be necessary to use up to ½ cup of the butter to hold ingredients together. Use the smaller measure with thinner peanut butter.

PEANUT BUTTER BALLS /HIGH

Make recipe for Peanut Butter Candy. Roll mixture into 1-inch balls. Let set 2 hours. Using toothpicks to hold balls, dip into melted chocolate. If chocolate begins to thicken, microwave another 10 to 15 seconds. Makes 60 balls.

Index

Pictured opposite
Peanut Butter Candy
Peanut Butter Balls
(page 61)

Glossary

Arcing: sparks seen in the microwave oven while it is operating. This is caused by using a utensil that contains metal. The spark results when a microwave hits the metal, discharging static electricity.

Browning: refers to the color of the food after it has been microwaved. Browning occurs naturally in a microwave oven only in meat over 3 pounds (see introduction to meat section).

Browning skillet: a special skillet designed for use in microwave ovens. It contains a special metal oxide enclosed in the base which is energy absorbing. When heated empty 4½ minutes, the metal element can become as hot as 450°.

Carry-over cooking: cooking which occurs in the food after the oven is turned off. The molecules of the food continue vibrating for a period of time equal to 1½ times the microwave time continuing to cook the food.

Cooking levels: the amount of time in seconds per minute that the microwave oven is emitting microwaves. At "high" or full power, the oven emits microwaves 100 percent of the time. At defrost or medium cycle, the oven emits microwaves only 30 seconds every minute, resting the remaining 30 seconds. During this period, the microwaves produced in the first 30 seconds penetrate farther into the food without more waves being added. Low power is usually 20 seconds of microwave emission per minute.

Density: refers to the porousness of the food. The lighter foods, such as bread, absorb microwave energy faster than less porous items, such as meat. The more dense the food, the longer cooking time required.

Piercing: poking a small hole into an item or its vacuum-packed container with a fork, knife or even a toothpick to allow steam to escape. Cooking pouches, potatoes, chicken livers, squash and egg yolks are examples of items that should be pierced.

Rearranging: moving large pieces of food after part of the cooking time has elapsed, from the outer edge of the dish toward the center, and those in the center to the outside. This ensures evenness of microwave power.

Shielding: covering certain items with a thin layer of foil which deflects microwaves away from the area shielded. Shielding is done to eliminate overcooking portions of meat thinner than the rest, or when cooking cakes in square and rectangular pans.

Standing time: the time after the food has finished its microwave cooking and the action of the food molecules continue traveling to the center of the food, thus finishing the cooking at the center.

Stirring: moving food with a spoon after part of the cooking time has elapsed so that the portion of food at the center of the dish goes toward the outer edge and that on the outside moves to the center. All food then gets an equal distribution of microwaves.

Turning: changing position of the dish by a one-quarter or one-half turn after part of the cooking time has elapsed. This is necessary for evenness of heat distribution. Turning is done when the food cannot be disturbed as in stirring.

Volume: the amount of food in the oven. As the volume doubles, the cooking time is increased 1½ times.

Undercooking: microwaving the food to a degree that it is not quite done. The standing time will then finish cooking it.